Paul Morris

Skill Area: Vocabulary
Ages: 10-18
Grades: 5-12

LinguiSystems, Inc.
3100 4th Avenue
East Moline, IL 61244-9300
1-800 PRO IDEA
1-800-776-4332

FAX: 1-800-577-4555
E-mail: service@linguisystems.com
Web: www.linguisystems.com
TDD: 1-800-933-8331
(for those with hearing impairments)

Copyright © 2004 LinguiSystems, Inc.

All of our products are copyrighted to protect the fine work of our authors. You may copy the worksheets as needed for your own use with students or clients. Any other reproduction or distribution of the pages in this book is prohibited, including copying the entire product to use as another primary source or "master" copy.

Printed in the U.S.A.

ISBN 0-7606-0532-7

About the Author

Paul Morris, M.S., CCC-SLP, has worked in a variety of public school settings for the past seven years. Since graduating from Central Missouri State University, he has worked in schools in Oregon and in the Clark County School District in Las Vegas, Nevada. Paul has a special interest in working with late elementary and secondary students with language delays.

101 Language Activities is Paul's first publication with LinguiSystems.

Dedication

To my incredibly supportive wife, Teresa, and to my beautiful son, Anderson. You both mean everything to me.

Table of Contents

Introduction 4

Adjectives
   Introduction 6
   Describe It 7
   Your Best Language 10
   Pie Charts 12
   Grid Activities 16

Antonyms/Synonyms
   Introduction 18
   Say it Again 19
   Grid Activities 23
   Pie Charts 26

Attributes and Functions
   Introduction 30
   Describe It 32
   Your Best Language 40
   Cross Out 42
   Grid Activities 48
   Pie Charts 52

Categories
   Introduction 56
   Be Specific 58
   Describe It 63
   Cross Out 65
   Grid Activities 67
   Pie Charts 69

Comparisons
   Introduction 72
   Describe It 73
   Your Best Language 76
   Grid Activities 79

Describing and Defining
   Introduction 84
   Describe It 86
   Your Best Language 90
   Grid Activities 95
   Pie Charts 99

Paraphrasing
   Introduction 102
   Say it Again 103
   Your Best Language 109
   Grid Activities 115

Answer Key 117
References 125

Introduction

Repetition is a key factor in reading instruction, and repetition is also necessary for successful language acquisition. One hurdle children with language learning disorders must overcome is a lack of interest in practicing skills that require repetition for effective learning. Varying exposures to essential language acquisition skills, as well as varying the means of repetition, is a valuable way to learn difficult language skills.

One difference between successful and unsuccessful reading and language achievement is that practicing in isolation is not a helpful means to learn language. Normally developing children learn language only through repeated exposure to and practice with language in different contexts. The same is true with children with language learning difficulties.

The varied activities in this book are meant to promote the skills necessary to communicate effectively in the classroom. Too often, children with language difficulties simply give up when faced with a challenging task. Kids with communication deficits often simply remain quiet when asked to explain their knowledge, even when that knowledge exists. For some children, language is a wonderful tool that can open countless doors, while for others, it stands as a frustrating wall between themselves and the rest of the world. The activities in this book are meant to chip away at that wall.

How to Use this Book

Each chapter begins with a short introduction that includes these elements:

- **Types of Activities:** an overview of the activities included in the chapter and additional instructions for their use
- **IEP Goals and Objectives:** sample IEP goals to guide your instruction and aid accountability
- **Statements to Motivate:** brief statements to share with your students in order to help them understand the importance of the skill and the rationale for practicing it

101 Language Activities is organized by language goal areas with similar activities divided into separate chapters. While some minimal explanations are included on many of the worksheets, the instructions required for a language impaired student to understand the concepts tend to be effective when presented orally with individualized modifications.

The activities in this book are not meant to be used exclusively. They are most beneficial when used as supplementary material to increase understanding and for repetition after the instructor has introduced the target concept through other means.

Introduction, continued

Vocabulary and the Curriculum

Vocabulary words from the curriculum have been integrated into each activity. The words included in *101 Language Activities* are intended to be representative of words that students throughout the United States should know. For kids who are specifically working on vocabulary, these words may be a starting point. For example, an instructor can try to discuss the word *government* with a fifth-grader and quickly ascertain that student's level of knowledge with this fourth-grade curriculum word. If the student is able to associate words such as *vote* or *leaders* with *government*, then it's not necessary to work on that word. If, however, the student has no clue what *government* is, targeted practice with that word is necessary. Activities such as the ones in this book will provide another situation in which the student can talk about specific vocabulary and associated words. Students with language learning difficulties often need additional practice using and understanding vocabulary expected to be mastered at much younger grades.

Because the acquisition and successful use of separate language skills are so interdependent on other skills, it is often beneficial to address an area even when it is not a direct target of daily practice. Research has consistently shown that retention of material is greatly improved when the timing of stimulus presentations are spread out rather than presented at one time. This phenomenon, known as the spacing effect, "has been observed in virtually every experimental learning paradigm, and with all sorts of traditional research materials" (Dempster & Farris, 1990, p. 97).

Tips for Using the Activities

Some of the activities in this book are competitive. Competition is a great motivator, but it is often necessary to manipulate activities so that weaker participants don't feel bad about losing and stronger participants don't lose track of the purpose of the activity. One good way to do this is to stop the activity just before either person has had a chance to actually win.

Often children will dispute an answer. This is good — as long as the argument is reasonable and not excessive. It means that the student is developing important skills in critical thinking and persuasion. If the student can make a valid point and offer support for that point, then credit should be given.

Many of the activities are intended to be challenging. Students often will not be able to dive right in and be successful without prior preparation. It is generally effective to quickly discuss some of the concepts ahead of time so students will have a greater chance of success with an activity. Encourage your students to use good thinking skills, along with trial and error, to complete these activities

Have fun!

Adjectives — Introduction

Types of Activities

- **Describe It** (pages 7-9)
  These activities help students explore the breadth and limitation of certain adjectives. Assist students who may have difficulty with this activity to see that certain words can be used to describe more than one thing. The matching activity on page 9 may be particularly challenging, because there is really only one way that all the words can be used once. Encourage discussion about this activity, as many students will have their own opinions about these adjectives and their uses.

- **Your Best Language** (pages 10-11)
  These activities challenge your students to provide two adjectives to describe each item. The goal of these activities is to use accurate, specific language.

- **Pie Charts** (pages 12-15)
  In the first two pie charts, students are challenged to match one adjective with a noun. In the final two charts, students choose two adjectives for each noun. Remind students that each adjective can only be used once. Encourage them to scrutinize their choices and use trial and error to complete the activity.

- **Grid Activities** (pages 16-17)
  These grids are set up as game boards. Have students use tokens and a die to move around the board. When a student lands on a word, challenge him to name an object that the adjective describes. To increase the difficulty, have players name two or more items each adjective describes. Use this versatile format in any way that works best for you and your students.

IEP Goals and Objectives:

- The student will identify adjectives, when provided multiple choices and foils, that can accurately describe curriculum content words with 90% accuracy.
- The student will use appropriate adjectives to describe vocabulary words with 90% accuracy.
- The student will include correct adjectives when defining curriculum-relevant vocabulary words with 80% accuracy.
- The student will use grade- and age-appropriate adjectives in sentences with 80% accuracy.

Statements to Motivate

- The more adjectives you know, the better your verbal and written language will be.
- Using adjectives correctly helps people know exactly what you are writing and talking about.
- Adjectives help your writing and speaking to be more colorful, interesting, and precise.

adjectives 1

describe it

Adjectives help you describe things. The more adjectives you know and use, the more accurate your speaking and writing will be.

▲ Circle all the words that can describe a **story character**.

▲ Underline all the words that can describe **gasoline**.

▲ Put a box around all the words that can describe the **plot of a story**.

▲ Cross out all the words that can describe a **homework assignment**.

Note: You should mark all the words at least once. Some words may be marked more than once.

short	liquid	easy
imaginary	confusing	difficult
smelly	dangerous	mysterious
scary	helpful	expensive
educational	tall	long

adjectives 2

describe it

Adjectives help you describe things. The more adjectives you know and use, the more accurate your speaking and writing will be.

▲ Circle all the words that can describe an **explorer**.

▲ Underline all the words that can describe a **patient in a hospital**.

▲ Put a box around all the words that can describe a **political candidate**.

▲ Cross out all the words that can describe a **piece of candy**.

Note: You should mark all the words at least once. Some words may be marked more than once.

tired	strong	weak
sick	brilliant	intelligent
brave	sweet	busy
unhealthy	curious	sticky
interesting	tricky	gooey

101 Language Activities   Copyright © 2004 LinguiSystems, Inc.

adjectives 3

describe it

You can often describe something better if you use more than one adjective.

→ Draw lines to connect an adjective from each column that could describe each noun. An example is done for you. Be careful — there is only one right way to use each adjective.

adjectives	nouns	adjectives
smelly	story character	scary
curious	story plot	tricky
sweet	gasoline	intelligent
educational	homework assignment	difficult
imaginary	explorer	expensive
mysterious	hospital patient	brave
unhealthy	political candidate	sticky
busy	piece of candy	weak

(Example line connects imaginary — story character — tricky)

multiple adjectives 4

your best language

Adjectives help you describe things. The more adjectives you know and use, the more accurate your speaking and writing will be. Here's an example of how using more than one adjective can make a definition more accurate:

What is a dictionary?

OK	Good	Great
(no adjectives)	*(1 adjective)*	*(2 adjectives)*
a book	a **big** book	a **big reference** book

A dictionary is a **big reference** book.

➡ Write two adjectives to describe each noun.

1. Oil is a _____ _____ substance.

2. A violin is a _____ _____ instrument.

3. A city is a _____ _____ place.

4. A concert is a _____ _____ event.

5. Uranium is a _____ _____ element.

6. A blink is a _____ _____ action.

7. The Panama Canal is a _____ _____ waterway.

8. A computer is a _____ _____ machine.

9. A roller coaster is a _____ _____ ride.

10. Steel is a _____ _____ material.

multiple adjectives 5

your best language

Adjectives help you describe things. The more adjectives you know and use, the more accurate your speaking and writing will be. Here's an example of how using more than one adjective can make a definition more accurate:

What is a sweater?

OK	Good	Great
(no adjectives)	*(1 adjective)*	*(2 adjectives)*
clothing	**warm** clothing	**warm winter** clothing

A sweater is **warm winter** clothing.

→ Write two adjectives to describe each noun.

1. The Arctic is a _____ _____ place.

2. An iceberg is a _____ _____ formation.

3. A flag is a _____ _____ symbol.

4. Celery is a _____ _____ vegetable.

5. The Earth's crust is a _____ _____ layer of rock.

6. The Amazon is a _____ _____ river.

7. Thanksgiving is a _____ _____ holiday.

8. Paper is a _____ _____ material.

9. A telephone is a _____ _____ device.

10. A finger is a _____ _____ body part.

adjectives 6

pie charts

→ Choose the adjective and noun pair that go best together and write them on the lines below.

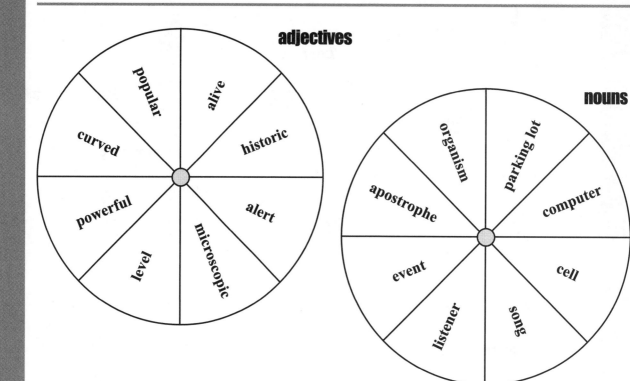

adjectives

nouns

adjective	**noun**
1. _____	_____
2. _____	_____
3. _____	_____
4. _____	_____
5. _____	_____
6. _____	_____
7. _____	_____
8. _____	_____

101 Language Activities Copyright © 2004 LinguiSystems, Inc.

pie charts

adjectives | 7

→ Choose the adjective and noun pair that go best together and write them on the lines below.

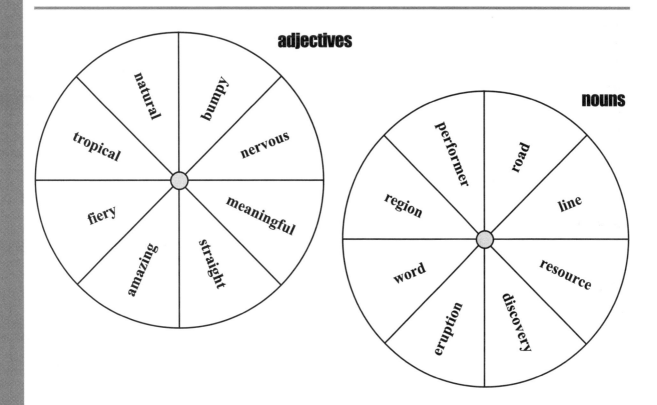

adjectives: natural, bumpy, nervous, meaningful, straight, amazing, fiery, tropical

nouns: performer, road, line, resource, discovery, eruption, word, region

adjective	noun
1. _____	_____
2. _____	_____
3. _____	_____
4. _____	_____
5. _____	_____
6. _____	_____
7. _____	_____
8. _____	_____

adjectives 8

pie charts

→ Choose two adjectives that best describe each noun and write all three words on the lines below.

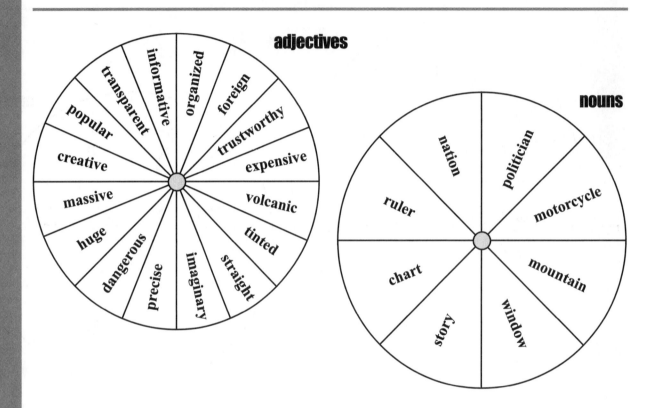

adjectives wheel: transparent, informative, organized, foreign, trustworthy, expensive, volcanic, tinted, straight, imaginary, precise, dangerous, huge, massive, creative, popular

nouns wheel: nation, politician, motorcycle, mountain, window, story, chart, ruler

noun	adjective 1	adjective 2
1. _____	_____	_____
2. _____	_____	_____
3. _____	_____	_____
4. _____	_____	_____
5. _____	_____	_____
6. _____	_____	_____
7. _____	_____	_____
8. _____	_____	_____

101 Language Activities — Copyright © 2004 LinguiSystems, Inc.

adjectives 9

pie charts

→ Choose two adjectives that best describe each noun and write all three words on the lines below.

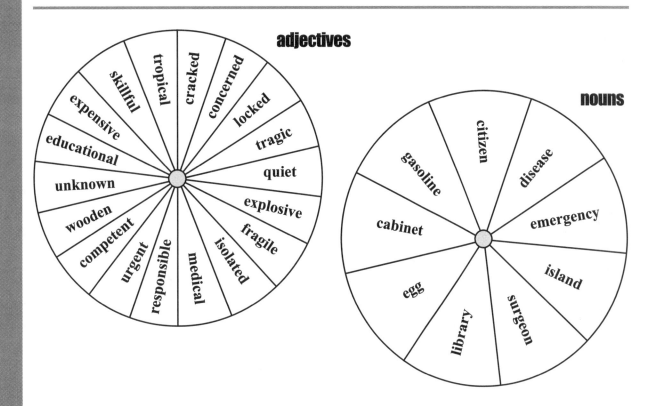

adjectives

(wheel): tropical, cracked, concerned, locked, tragic, quiet, explosive, fragile, isolated, medical, responsible, urgent, competent, wooden, unknown, educational, expensive, skillful

nouns

(wheel): citizen, disease, emergency, island, surgeon, library, egg, cabinet, gasoline

noun	adjective 1	adjective 2
1. _____	_____	_____
2. _____	_____	_____
3. _____	_____	_____
4. _____	_____	_____
5. _____	_____	_____
6. _____	_____	_____
7. _____	_____	_____
8. _____	_____	_____
9. _____	_____	_____

adjectives 10

grid activity

→ See the directions on page 6.

transparent	precious	flat	volcanic	thin
nervous	imaginary	bright	bumpy	ancient
important	creative	different	helpful	real
warm	cracked	complicated	wide	dangerous
unbelievable	tropical	ordinary	heavy	extinct
weak	unknown	fragile	sick	unhealthy
forgetful	friendly	awake	explosive	wooden

adjectives 11

grid activity

→ See the directions on page 6.

silent	educational	ancient	unknown	complex
shallow	important	bright	quiet	historic
microscopic	popular	smooth	round	special
careful	sticky	intelligent	straight	transparent
popular	calm	sore	expensive	solid
liquid	busy	simple	strong	essential
natural	tired	purple	imaginary	skillful

Antonyms and Synonyms – Introduction

Types of Activities

- **Say It Again** (pages 19-22)
  Synonym substitution is a crucial metalinguistic skill. Using synonyms correctly allows students to paraphrase and comprehend information successfully. These pages will help students practice identifying synonym pairs in context.

- **Grid Activities** (pages 23-25)
  These pages can be used in a variety of ways. Students can simply locate the pairs of synonyms and antonyms in these grids and list them on another sheet of paper. You may also present the activity as a competitive game. Provide game tokens and a die, and then choose a direction for students to move around the grid (top to bottom, side to side). When a player lands on a word on the grid, she finds the other half of its pair on the board and writes her initials in each box on the grid. The game continues until all the boxes on the grid have been initialed. (As students roll the die and move, have them skip over boxes that have already been initialed.)

- **Pie Charts** (pages 26-29)
  In these activities, students are challenged to match synonym and antonym pairs. Remind students that each word can only be used once. Encourage them to scrutinize their choices and use trial and error to complete the activity.

IEP Goals and Objectives:

- The student will identify grade- and age-appropriate antonyms and synonyms with 90% accuracy.
- The student will label grade- and age-appropriate antonyms and synonyms with 80% accuracy.
- The student will accurately substitute synonyms in context with 80% accuracy.
- The student will identify correct paraphrasing of sentences/paragraphs with 90% accuracy.

Statements to Motivate

- Synonyms and antonyms help make your verbal and written language more expressive and creative.
- If a word is on the tip of your tongue but you can't find it, use the word's synonym instead.
- There are often many ways to say the same thing. Your reading and verbal comprehension will be better if you know different ways of saying the same thing. You're more likely to understand what you are reading and what others are saying.

synonyms 12

say it again

You can use different words to say the same thing. Two words that mean about the same are called *synonyms*.

→ Underline the word in each sentence that can be replaced by the synonym in the right-hand column. The first one is done for you.

1. The book's <u>conclusion</u> was lengthy.   ending

2. My estimate of the answer was correct.   guess

3. Round your solution to the nearest whole number.   answer

4. Your belief about a subject is not always right.   opinion

5. Eight is more than three.   greater

6. The magician made the rabbit disappear.   vanish

7. Her community is nice and quiet.   neighborhood

8. The location for the movie *Star Wars* is outer space.   setting

9. Thomas Edison was the creator of many things.   inventor

10. I didn't make one mistake on the math test.   error

synonyms 13

say it again

You can use different words to say the same thing. Two words that mean about the same are called *synonyms*.

→ Underline the word in each sentence that can be replaced by the synonym in the right-hand column. The first one is done for you.

1. The book's conclusion was <u>lengthy</u>.   long

2. My estimate of the answer was correct.   right

3. I compared the giraffe to the tall tree.   high

4. Round your answer to the nearest whole number.   closest

5. The volume of the Pacific Ocean is huge.   enormous

6. Your speech rate should not be too fast or too slow. quick

7. The knife's edge is blunt.   dull

8. It is not always appropriate to voice your opinion. relevant

9. The investment in computer stock was profitable.   rewarding

10. The candidates were nervous on election night.   anxious

synonyms 14

say it again

→ Pick a word from the box that can replace a word in each sentence. Write the word on the line next to the sentence. Then underline the word in the sentence the synonym can replace. An example is done for you.

below	plan
careful	mistake
gift	~~rescued~~
evidence	empty
author	spotless

1. The fire fighter ~~saved~~ the cat.   *rescued*

2. The squirrel ran under the bridge. _____

3. We moved into the vacant apartment. _____

4. Our teacher made an error in her calculations. _____

5. The writer had a large vocabulary. _____

6. The Statue of Liberty was a present from France. _____

7. Please be gentle with that egg. _____

8. We scrubbed the counter until it was clean. _____

9. The prosecutor collected enough information to convict the criminal. _____

10. My test-taking strategy helped me earn a good grade. _____

synonyms 15

say it again

→ Pick a word from the box that can replace a word in each sentence. Write the word on the line next to the sentence. Then underline the word in the sentence the synonym can replace.

ancient	intelligent
entire	bent
obvious	paper
nations	entrance
together	several

1. The outline had many words. _____

2. He ate the whole chicken for dinner. _____

3. Millions of years ago, the continents were joined. _____

4. That old, crooked tree should be cut down. _____

5. Scientists study old civilizations. _____

6. Write your name at the top of your sheet. _____

7. Oil is found in many countries. _____

8. Albert Einstein was extremely smart. _____

9. The answer to the professor's question was clear. _____

10. There was only one access to the theater. _____

synonyms 16

grid activity

→ This grid contains 20 pairs of synonyms. Write each pair on another sheet of paper. See additional ideas for using this page on page 18.

vacant	beneath	saved	crooked	little
furious	vanish	container	exchange	liberty
wealthy	present	trade	nation	rich
angry	disappear	reply	holder	writer
gift	hide	rescued	error	freedom
answer	spotless	small	smart	conceal
mistake	author	country	bent	below
intelligent	empty	clean	pick	choose

antonyms 17

grid activity

→ This grid contains 20 pairs of antonyms. Write each pair on another sheet of paper. See additional ideas for using this page on page 18.

broken	cloudy	reward	energetic	outside
arrive	lazy	bumpy	first	punish
safe	interesting	light	open	rough
avoid	new	subtract	seek	friend
dark	enemy	build	dangerous	fixed
close	more	flat	leave	boring
smooth	add	sunny	inside	light
destroy	last	heavy	ancient	less

antonyms & synonyms

grid activity

→ Write either an antonym or a synonym for each word on another sheet of paper. See additional ideas for using this page on page 18.

conceal	broken	start	solemn	demolish
silly	negative	nervous	beginning	hide
diverse	request	similar	enter	leave
proud	different	serious	positive	conclusion
pessimistic	exit	build	ridiculous	fixed
operational	destroy	helpful	hinder	assist
obstruct	insecure	seek	help	construct
arrive	end	search	confident	alike

synonyms 19

pie charts

→ Choose a word from each wheel that makes a synonym pair. Write the pairs below. The first one is done for you.

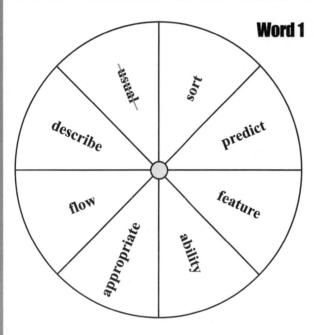
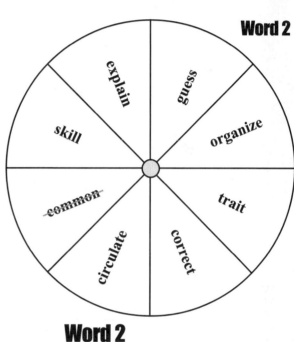

Word 1 wheel contains: usual, sort, predict, feature, ability, appropriate, flow, describe

Word 2 wheel contains: explain, guess, organize, trait, correct, circulate, common, skill

	Word 1	Word 2
1.	usual	common
2.		
3.		
4.		
5.		
6.		
7.		
8.		

synonyms | 20

pie charts

→ Choose a word from each wheel that makes a synonym pair. Write the pairs below.

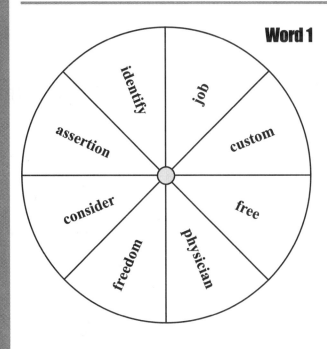
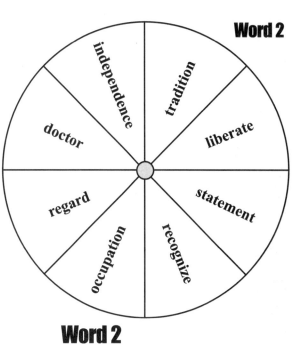

Word 1   Word 2

1. _____   _____
2. _____   _____
3. _____   _____
4. _____   _____
5. _____   _____
6. _____   _____
7. _____   _____
8. _____   _____

antonyms 21

pie charts

→ Choose a word from each wheel that makes an antonym pair. Write the pairs below. The first one is done for you.

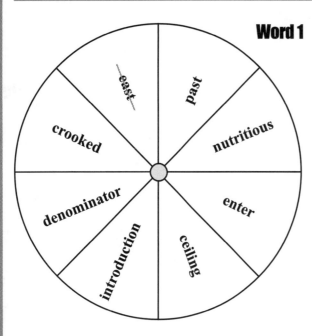
Word 1: east, past, nutritious, enter, ceiling, introduction, denominator, crooked

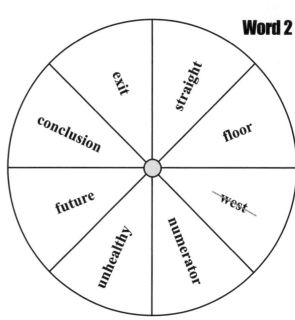
Word 2: exit, straight, floor, west, numerator, unhealthy, future, conclusion

	Word 1	Word 2
1.	east	west
2.		
3.		
4.		
5.		
6.		
7.		
8.		

antonyms 22

pie charts

→ Choose a word from each wheel that makes an antonym pair. Write the pairs below.

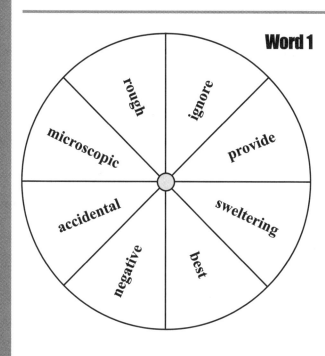

Word 1

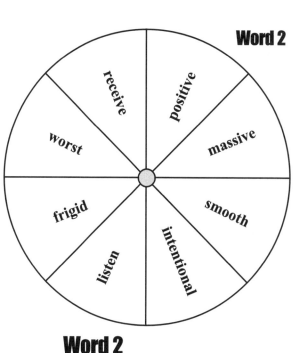

Word 2

Word 1	Word 2
1. _____	_____
2. _____	_____
3. _____	_____
4. _____	_____
5. _____	_____
6. _____	_____
7. _____	_____
8. _____	_____

Attributes and Functions – Introduction

Types of Activities

- **Describe It** (pages 32-39)
  These activities help students see how multiple items can have common attributes and functions. Encourage discussion about these activities as many students will have their own opinions about how these pages can be completed.

- **Your Best Language** (pages 40-41)
  These activities challenge your students to use their knowledge of attributes and functions to provide items that match the descriptions. There may be more than one correct answer for each item. Encourage students to complete the pages independently and then share their results with one another.

- **Cross Out** (pages 42-47)
  These flexible activities can be used in a variety of ways to show students how various attributes and functions can be shared by certain items or are exclusive to other items. The printed directions suggest having a reader randomly read directions from the bottom of the page while the student crosses out pictures or items that match the directions. Another way to use this page is to have the student roll two dice and follow the direction of the corresponding number shown on the dice roll. The student continues throwing the dice and crossing out items until all items have been marked. You will surely find other ways to use these pages.

- **Grid Activities** (pages 48-51)
  These pages can be used in a variety of ways. Students can randomly select an item on the grid and name an object that matches the attributes or functions listed. You may also present the activity as a competitive game. Provide game tokens and a die, and then choose a direction for students to move around the grid (top to bottom, side to side). When a player lands on a word on the grid, he names an item that contains the printed attribute or function. The player writes his initials on the box on the grid. The game continues until all the boxes on the grid have been initialed. (As students roll the die and move, have them skip over boxes that have already been initialed.)

- **Pie Charts** (pages 52-55)
  These pages challenge students to match one attribute or function from each pie chart to an item at the top of the page. You might have your students simply list the items on another sheet of paper and write a single attribute or function from each pie chart that describes the item. A more visual approach to the activity is to have students assign a different pattern (stripes, polka dots), color, or number to each item at the top of the page and mark the box with that designation. The student then uses the same pattern, color, or number to mark the section of each pie chart that goes with the item. Only one section of each chart goes with an item. An example of a completed pie chart is shown on the following page. This student has chosen to use different patterns, but numbers or colors will probably be easier for most students.

IEP Goals and Objectives:

- The student will identify and label attributes and functions of curriculum-relevant vocabulary words with 90% accuracy.
- The student will label examples of words with curriculum-relevant attributes and functions with 90% accuracy.
- The student will label multiple attributes and functions of curriculum content words with 80% accuracy.
- The student will label curriculum-relevant vocabulary words given attributes and/or functions with 80% accuracy.

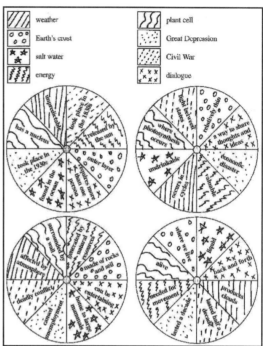

Statements to Motivate

- In order to succeed at these activities (and in school) you should pay close attention to the details.
- Using attributes and functions to describe words will help people know exactly what you're talking about.
- Ask yourself, "What does it look like" or "What parts does it have" to determine an object's attributes. Then ask, "What does it do?" or "What is it used for" to find its functions.

attributes and functions

describe it

Nouns can be important attributes. They tell you about the parts that make up something.

▲ Circle anything that is in the **U.S. Constitution**.

▲ Underline anything you can find in **North America**.

▲ Put a box around anything that can be **revised**.

▲ Cross out anything that can be **confirmed**.

Note: You should mark all the words at least once. Some words may be marked more than once.

report	valley	problems
rights	paragraph	features
opinion	proposal	vision
fact	oil	story
amendment	freedom	nation

101 Language Activities

attributes and functions | 24

describe it

Nouns can be important attributes. They tell you about the parts that make up something.

▲ Circle anything that goes through a **cycle**.

▲ Underline anything that can be **organized**.

▲ Put a box around anything that can be found in the **Earth's crust**.

▲ Cross out anything that is a part of **politics**.

Note: You should mark all the words at least once. Some words may be marked more than once.

election	energy	soil
campaign	season	copper
year	uranium	promise
debate	life	weather
government	research	erosion

attributes and functions | 25

describe it

Verbs can be important functions. They tell you what something does.

▲ Circle anything that a **paragraph** does.
▲ Underline anything that a **scientist** can do.
▲ Put a box around anything that a **planet** does.
▲ Cross out every action done by a **magnet**.

Note: You should mark all the words at least once. Some words may be marked more than once.

describe   pull   apply

define   communicate   attract

observe   revolve   experiment

rotate   spin   explain

repel   learn   investigate

attributes and functions | **26**

describe it

Verbs can be important functions. They tell you what something does.

▲ Circle anything that a **river** does.

▲ Underline anything that a **muscle** does.

▲ Put a box around anything that can be done with a **chart**.

▲ Cross out every action that can be done by a **judge**.

Note: You should mark all the words at least once. Some words may be marked more than once.

erode	react	compare
persuade	decide	interpret
organize	question	relax
flex	contract	saturate
flow	blink	overflow

attributes and functions 27

describe it

Attributes and functions help you describe and recognize things.

▲ Circle anything that is **industrial**.

▲ Underline anything that can **focus**.

▲ Put a box around anything that has a **base**.

▲ Cross out every item that can **store** something.

▲ Put a star by anything that carries **current**.

Note: You should mark all the pictures at least once. Some pictures may be marked more than once.

attributes and functions 28

describe it

Attributes and functions help you describe and recognize things.

▲ Circle anything that shows something **healthy**.

▲ Underline anything that has to do with **politics**.

▲ Put a box around anything that is a type of **energy**.

▲ Cross out every item that is **light**.

▲ Put a star by anything that can **open**.

Note: You should mark all the pictures at least once. Some pictures may be marked more than once.

attributes and functions

describe it

More than one item can often have the same attribute. For example, both a chair and a cabinet can be made of wood.

→ Draw a circle around the items on the right that fit each description.

1. contains information   computer   car   encyclopedia

2. has strings   violin   piano   cherry

3. has rings   Saturn   hand   iced tea

4. is valuable   sculpture   painting   paper clip

5. can be bright   student   kite   light bulb

6. can be full   mouth   bus   apple

7. has legs   baby   worm   table

8. has a stem   flower   cherry   pen

9. has many colors   rainbow   sunset   fire truck

10. has a flat top   mesa   head   table

attributes and functions 30

describe it

More than one thing can often have the same function. For example, you can wipe a table with both a sponge and a rag.

→ Draw a circle around the items on the right that fit each description.

1. helps you do homework		pencil		soda		brain

2. can break			vase		bone		penny

3. used to communicate		mouth		shoe		telephone

4. helps you find your way		tissue		map		compass

5. can be chewed			steak		gum		glass of milk

6. protects your head		sweater		helmet		umbrella

7. used to buy things		credit card	check		library card

8. grow best outdoors		tomatoes	trees		flowers

9. used to get rid of a stain		gelatin		bleach		detergent

10. used after a shower		towel		soap		deodorant

101 Language Activities	Copyright © 2004 LinguiSystems, Inc.

attributes and functions | 31

your best language

Sometimes you can describe something by what it *is not*.
Here's an example:

> It's a hard part of your finger but it *isn't* a bone.
> *fingernail*

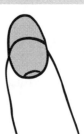

→ Write an item that fits each description. There may be more than one correct answer for each.

1. It's something you can chew, but you don't swallow. _____

2. It has a shell, but it isn't an animal. _____

3. It has tusks, but it isn't an elephant. _____

4. It's used to measure length, but it isn't a ruler. _____

5. It has horns, but it isn't an animal. _____

6. It's a liquid people drink, but it's not good for them. _____

7. It's a punctuation mark, but it never goes at the end of a sentence. _____

8. It's a continent, but it isn't attached to any other continent. _____

9. This person is a leader of a country, but the individual isn't elected. _____

10. It's a type of reference book, but it doesn't have many pictures. _____

11. It's a state in the western U.S., but it isn't on the coast or on the border with another country. _____

12. It's part of a book, but it isn't in the front. _____

101 Language Activities   **40**   Copyright © 2004 LinguiSystems, Inc.

attributes and functions 32

your best language

Sometimes you can describe something by what it *is not*. Here's an example:

It's a part of a classroom that can't be easily moved. *chalkboard*

➡ Write an item that fits each description. There may be more than one correct answer for each.

1. It's a large ocean creature, but it isn't a mammal. _____

2. It's a war the U.S. fought, but it wasn't on American soil. _____

3. It's something that helps a living thing breathe, but it isn't a lung. _____

4. It's a punctuation mark, but it is never in the middle of a sentence. _____

5. It's someone on the nightly news, but it isn't a reporter. _____

6. It's a part of a car, but it doesn't last a long time. _____

7. It's part of a story, but it isn't the character or setting. _____

8. It's a large body of water, but it doesn't contain saltwater. _____

9. It's something you pack for a long trip, but it isn't clothes. _____

10. It's an odd number, but it isn't a prime number. _____

11. It's a common pet, but it doesn't go outside. _____

12. It's a way to buy things, but it isn't cash or a check. _____

attributes and functions 33

cross out

Cut off the bottom of this page and give it to someone else. Have that person randomly read items to you as you cross out the pictures that are described until each picture is crossed out. See additional suggestions for using this page on page 30.

→ Cross out any animal:

1. with a shell
2. with horns/tusks
3. with wings
4. with hooves
5. with gills
6. with arms
7. with fins
8. with feathers
9. with claws
10. with a hump
11. without legs
12. that can sting

attributes and functions | 34

cross out

Cut off the bottom of this page and give it to someone else. Have that person randomly read items to you as you cross out the pictures that are described until each picture is crossed out. See additional suggestions for using this page on page 30.

→ Cross out any building or structure that:

1. has no roof
2. has an antenna
3. has a steeple
4. has no windows
5. has emergency exits
6. has a sign
7. is many stories tall
8. is not locked
9. is made of cloth
10. is used to communicate
11. can hold many people
12. holds only a few people

attributes and functions — 35

cross out

Cut off the bottom of this page and give it to someone else. Have that person randomly read items to you as you cross out the pictures that are described until each picture is crossed out. See additional suggestions for using this page on page 30.

➜ Cross out anything that is used to:

1. cook
2. improve vision
3. find a location
4. measure
5. transport people
6. communicate
7. buy products
8. make payments
9. help with math
10. protect your feet
11. determine weight
12. hold liquid

attributes and functions | 36

cross out

Cut off the bottom of this page and give it to someone else. Have that person randomly read items to you as you cross out the pictures that are described until each picture is crossed out. See additional suggestions for using this page on page 30.

➡ Cross out anything that:

1. travels on streets
2. requires a paddle
3. has no motor
4. has wings
5. has a windshield
6. has handlebars
7. uses sails
8. travels on tracks
9. travels off-road
10. has headlights
11. has a steering wheel
12. travels in the air

attributes and functions

cross out

Cut off the bottom of this page and give it to someone else. Have that person randomly read instructions to you as you cross out the items that are described until each item is crossed out. See additional suggestions for using this page on page 30.

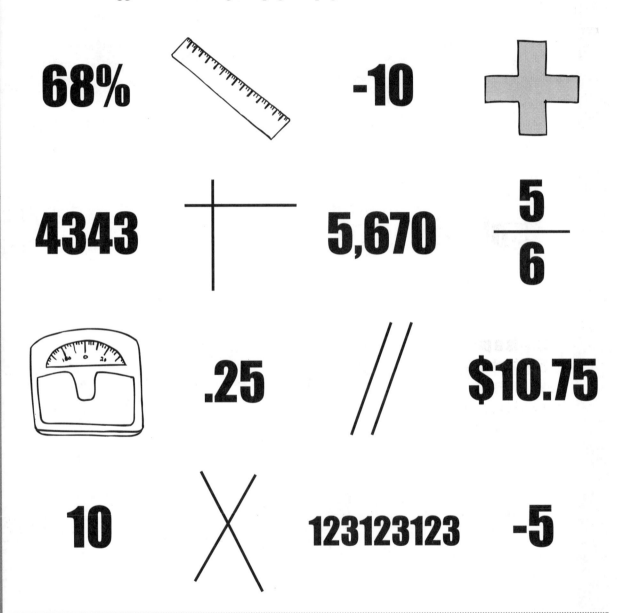

➜ Cross out any:
1. negative numbers
2. numbers with decimals
3. intersecting lines
4. parallel lines
5. fractions
6. objects that measure
7. math symbols
8. patterns
9. prices
10. percentages
11. odd numbers
12. even numbers

attributes and functions — 38

cross out

Cut off the bottom of this page and give it to someone else. Have that person randomly read instructions to you as you cross out the items that are described until each item is crossed out. See additional suggestions for using this page on page 30.

airplane   **Chicago**   **?**   **disgusting**

abbr.   **I went to the store, although I didn't want to.**   **flew**   **Can you help me?**

This is a paragraph. It is indented, and it contains sentences related to each other.   **old**   *Joe Schmoe*   **This sentence has a period.**

look   **I'll see.**   **Mr. King**

➔ Cross out any:

1. capitalized words
2. abbreviations
3. questions
4. statements
5. paragraphs
6. action words
7. describing words
8. punctuation
9. signatures
10. one-syllable words
11. two-syllable words
12. three-syllable words

attributes and functions

grid activity

→ See the directions on page 30.

has wings and feathers	has wheels and handlebars	is wet and clear	has ingredients and directions
has people and clapping	has states and cities	has doors and windows	has whiskers and paws
has planets, asteroids, and the sun	has houses, neighbors, and streets	has sharks, whales, sand, and fish	has numbers and hands
has floors, ceilings, doors, and walls	has a shade and a bulb	has a top, a middle, and a bottom	has teachers and students
has vowels and consonants	has rules, teams, and games	has a screen and remote control	has peanut butter, jelly, and bread
has a point and an eraser	has decimals, numbers, and buttons	has a windshield and steering wheel	has sleeves and a collar
has a title, pages, and a glossary	has aisles and cash registers	has legs, a back, and a seat	has leaves, bark, and branches

101 Language Activities

attributes and functions 40

grid activity

→ See the directions on page 30.

is an orange liquid	is solid and round	is a shape with angles	is a type of math problem with remainders
has voters and candidates	is green with an erasable, smooth surface	has mass	has cities and capitals
has legs and scales	has gears and moving parts	is a thin, flat object with lines	has a numerator and a denominator
has floors, teachers, and students	has faucets and drains	has red, yellow, and green lights	has petals and a stem
has drawers and handles	has a noun, a verb, and begins with a capital letter	is made of wax and has a wick	has a zipper and sleeves
has a monitor and keyboard	has many seats and four wheels	has a tail and is made of rock and ice	is made of metal and glass
has sand, sun, and surf	has an outline	has an apostrophe	has keys and strings

101 Language Activities — Copyright © 2004 LinguiSystems, Inc.

attributes and functions

grid activity

→ Write the number of each description by the word on the grid that matches it. An example is done for you.

1. helps you see tiny details
2. writes books
3. describes speed of speech
4. a state's leader
5. gets you from place to place
6. helps you find items in a book
7. organizes thoughts before writing
8. runs for public office
9. provides definitions of words
10. a person, place, or thing
11. the beginning of something
12. a guess you make
13. a way of doing something
14. describes a noun
15. ends a sentence
16. line that separates areas
17. measures items
18. a rule of behavior
19. helps you stay fit
20. an organization that makes a product

adjective	author	border	business
candidate	dictionary	exercise	governor
index	law	microscope 1	noun
outline	period	prediction	rate
ruler	source	strategy	transportation

attributes and functions

grid activity

→ See the directions on page 30.

helps students take tests	vibrates and produces sound	forms when sunlight falls on rain	a symbol that means "less than zero"
pulls things toward Earth	supports main ideas	erupts and causes damage	help you focus
people who tell us the news	tries to sell you things on TV	gives your body its shape	makes laws
reproduces	passes traits from one generation to another	makes a car move	keeps trains from derailing
makes discoveries	helps a car stop	event that gave the U.S. its freedom	is reusable
provides protection from disease	surrounds countries	helps us breathe	helps fish breathe
designs buildings	tries to get elected	compares things using like or as	shows you where to find things in a book
flows through arteries	slithers	has destructive, high winds	is in charge of a library
surrounds direct quotes	measures the power of an earthquake	explores space	tells what a word means
wakes people up on time	diagnoses and treats	helps you find your way	represents the entire Earth

attributes and functions | 43

pie charts

→ See the directions on page 30.

☐ weather   ☐ plant cell

☐ Earth's crust   ☐ Great Depression

☐ saltwater   ☐ Civil War

☐ energy   ☐ dialogue

Pie chart 1 (upper left) segments: unpredictable, took place in the 1830s, released by the sun, outer layer, requires more than one person, found in the ocean, took place in the 1930s, has a nucleus

Pie chart 2 (upper right) segments: fight between states, relatively thin, a way to share thoughts and ideas, economic disaster, valuable, occurs in cycles, undrinkable, where photosynthesis occurs

Pie chart 3 (lower left) segments: surrounded by a wall, generated by natural resources, made of rocks and soil, can be entertaining, home to large mammals, caused unemployment, deadly conflict, affected by atmosphere

Pie chart 4 (lower right) segments: where we live, liquid, back and forth, produces clouds, lasted half a decade, lasted a decade, needed for movement, alive

101 Language Activities   **52**   Copyright © 2004 LinguiSystems, Inc.

attributes and functions 44

pie charts

→ See the directions on page 30.

☐ echoes
☐ recycling
☐ the Universe
☐ fossils

☐ Gandhi
☐ Europe
☐ industry
☐ Mexico

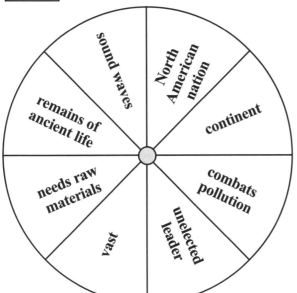
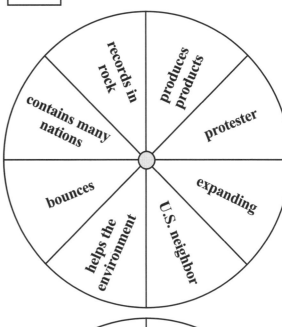
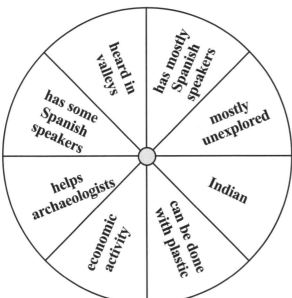
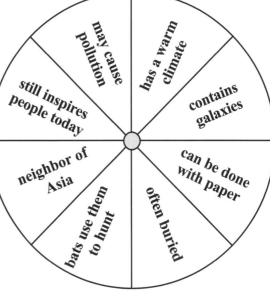

attributes and functions | 45

pie charts

→ See the directions on page 30.

☐ the brain
☐ language
☐ atom
☐ election

☐ Jupiter
☐ population
☐ newspaper
☐ magnetism

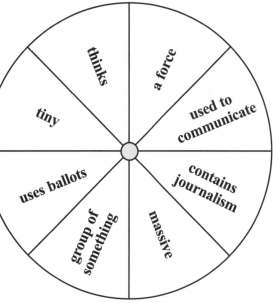
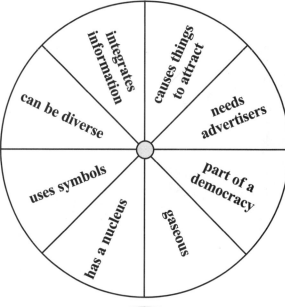

101 Language Activities — 54 — Copyright © 2004 LinguiSystems, Inc.

attributes and functions 46

pie charts

→ See the directions on page 30.

☐ freedom ☐ Internet

☐ President of the U.S. ☐ geometry

☐ history ☐ vocabulary

☐ business ☐ media

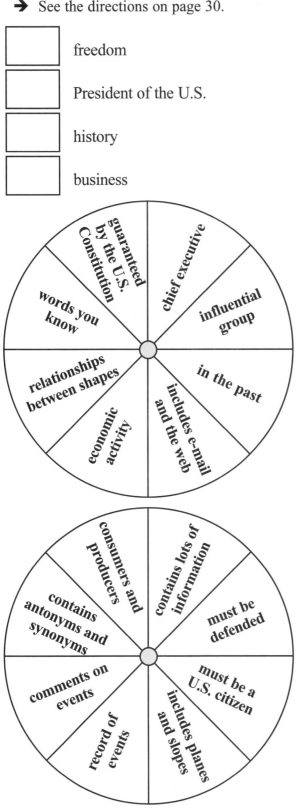
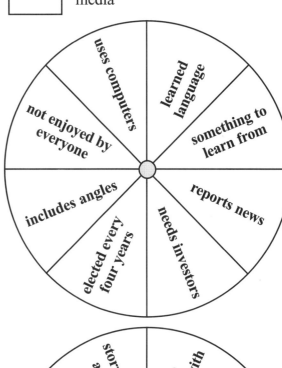
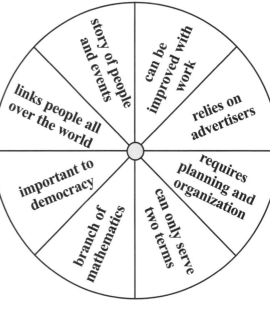

101 Language Activities   55   Copyright © 2004 LinguiSystems, Inc.

Categories – Introduction

Note: The categories targeted in this section are generally noun categories (furniture, symbols, etc.). Other types of categories, including adjectives and verbs, are addressed in the Adjectives *or* Attributes and Functions *sections.*

Types of Activities

- **Be Specific** (pages 58-62)
  These activities challenge your students to explore how categories and their items can move from the general (*large area*) to the specific (*Canada*). Word banks are provided to assist students, but if you wish to make the activities more challenging, cover these areas of the page when you photocopy the activities.

- **Describe It** (pages 63-64)
  These activities help students select items that belong to a specific category and to illustrate how some items may belong to more than one category.

- **Cross Out** (pages 65-66)
  These flexible activities can be used in a variety of ways to show students how various objects can belong to specific and shared categories. The printed directions suggest having a reader randomly read directions from the bottom of the page while the student crosses out the appropriate pictures. Another way to use this page is to have the student roll two dice and follow the direction of the corresponding number shown on the dice roll. The student continues throwing the dice and crossing out items until all items have been marked. You will surely find other ways to use these pages.

- **Grid Activities** (pages 67-68)
  These pages can be used in a variety of ways. Students can randomly select an item on the grid and name a predetermined number of items that matches the category listed. You may also present the activity as a competitive game. Provide game tokens and a die, and then choose a direction for students to move around the grid (top to bottom, side to side). When a player lands on a word on the grid, he names items that fit the category. The player writes his initials in the box on the grid. The game continues until all the boxes on the grid have been initialed. (As students roll the die and move, have them skip over boxes that have already been initialed.)

- **Pie Charts** (pages 69-71)
  These pages challenge students to match one item from each pie chart to the category at the top of the page. You might have your students simply list the category names on another sheet of paper and write a single item from each pie chart that fits the category. A more visual approach to the activity is to have students assign a different pattern (stripes, polka dots), color, or number to each category at the top of the page and mark the box with that designation. The student then uses the same pattern, color, or number to mark the item on each pie chart that goes with the category. Only one section of each chart goes with each category. An example of a completed pie chart for a similar activity is shown on page 31.

IEP Goals and Objectives:

- The student will name two or more members of limited set categories related to the curriculum with 80% accuracy.
- The student will identify categories of curriculum content words with 80% accuracy.
- The student will label the category when given two members of limited set categories related to the curriculum with 80% accuracy.
- The student will use categories and adjectives simultaneously to describe curriculum-relevant words with 80% accuracy.

Statements to Motivate

- If you are trying to describe something, begin by naming its category. Then you can compare it to other members of the category.
- Knowing categories and their members helps improve your creativity and your vocabulary. You can include more examples and details in your writing and speaking.
- Remembering words is easier when you know the categories they belong to because you can keep a larger set of related words in your head more efficiently.

categories 47

be specific

If you know the specific word that belongs to a category and its subcategories, you will use more accurate words in your writing and speaking.

→ Each line shows a general category in the left-hand column. The subcategories and describing words that follow tell you more information. Write the specific item from the box at the bottom that fits into the general category and its subcategories. An example is done for you.

General   **Specific**

1. large area   nation   U.S. neighbor   *Canada*

2. liquid   beverage   healthy   _____

3. person   man   inventor   _____

4. word   part of speech   describes nouns   _____

5. furniture   living room   has cushions   _____

6. time of year   season   warm   _____

7. emotion   positive   happy   _____

8. money   bill   small amount   _____

9. vacation spot   United States   resort   _____

10. food   snack   crunchy   _____

| adjective | spring | Disneyland | couch | Thomas Edison |
| milk | cheerful | one dollar | ~~Canada~~ | chips |

101 Language Activities   Copyright © 2004 LinguiSystems, Inc.

categories 48

be specific

If you know the specific word that belongs to a category and its subcategories, you will use more accurate words in your writing and speaking.

➜ Each line shows a general category in the left-hand column. The subcategories and describing words that follow tell you more information. Write the specific item that fits into the general category and its subcategories.

General   **Specific**

1. person   leader   president   _____

2. provides energy natural resource crude oil   _____

3. structure   building   tall   _____

4. seasoning   sweet   white   _____

5. instrument   woodwind   silver   _____

6. exercise   sport   racquet   _____

7. word   part of speech   action   _____

8. state   Southern   coastal   _____

9. food   breakfast   bread   _____

10. organism   animal   one-celled   _____

| Florida | skyscraper | gasoline | flute | amoeba |
| toast | George Bush | verb | sugar | tennis |

categories 49

be specific

If you know the category and subcategories a word belongs to, you can describe it better.

→ Each line shows a specific item in the right-hand column and the subcategories it belongs to. Write its general category from the box in the blank. See how the description moves from the general to the specific. The first one is done for you.

	General			**Specific**
1.	_food_	snack	cookie	Oreo
2.	_____	writing utensil	pencil	mechanical pencil
3.	_____	beverage	soda	root beer
4.	_____	female	relative	grandmother
5.	_____	change	coin	quarter
6.	_____	state	Midwest	Nebraska
7.	_____	subject	pronoun	she
8.	_____	round	three-dimensional	sphere
9.	_____	hard	building material	steel
10.	_____	Great Britain	England	London

city	liquid	~~food~~	U.S.A.	shape
school supply	person	money	word	metal

101 Language Activities   Copyright © 2004 LinguiSystems, Inc.

categories 50

be specific

If you know the category and subcategories a word belongs to, you can describe it better.

→ Each line shows a specific item in the right-hand column and the subcategories it belongs to. Write its general category from the box in the blank. See how the description moves from the general to the specific.

General			**Specific**
1. _____	has legs	chair	recliner
2. _____	household	cooling	air conditioner
3. _____	worn on feet	type of shoe	gym shoe
4. _____	student	wizard	Harry Potter
5. _____	season	cold	winter
6. _____	addition	symbol	plus sign
7. _____	has wheels	used in an emergency	ambulance
8. _____	beef	patty	hamburger
9. _____	percussion	shaken	maraca
10. _____	measures	temperature	thermometer

character	instrument	time of year	appliance	meat
math	furniture	device	vehicle	clothing

101 Language Activities — Copyright © 2004 LinguiSystems, Inc.

categories | 51

be specific

If you know the specific word that belongs to a category and its subcategories, you will use more accurate words in your writing and speaking.

➔ Each line shows a general category in the left-hand column and a specific item on the right. Fill in a subcategory name or description from the box that completes the "chain" from general to specific. The first one is done for you.

General   **Specific**

1. word — *part of speech* — describes verbs — adverb
2. activity — sport — _____ — golf
3. furniture — _____ — mattress — bed
4. person — woman — _____ — Amelia Earhart
5. food — _____ — vegetable — broccoli
6. liquid — beverage — _____ — soda
7. landmark — _____ — Paris — Eiffel Tower
8. holiday — winter — _____ — Valentine's Day
9. nation — _____ — island — Cuba
10. emotion — negative — _____ — sad

| small | individual | pilot | unhappy | bedroom |
| ~~part of speech~~ | unhealthy | February | healthy | Europe |

categories 52

describe it

Some items can belong to more than one category. Follow the directions to mark the items on the page. Each item will be marked once. Some items will have more than one mark.

▲ Draw a circle around each picture that shows an **animal**.

▲ Draw a box around each picture that shows a **container**.

▲ Draw a wavy line under each picture that shows a **healthy food**.

▲ Draw straight line under each picture that shows something **unhealthy**.

▲ Draw an X over each picture that shows some type of **chemical**.

▲ Draw a triangle around each picture that shows a **snack**.

101 Language Activities

categories 53

describe it

Some items can belong to more than one category. Follow the directions to mark the items on the page. Each item will be marked once. Some items will have more than one mark.

▲ Draw a circle around each picture that shows a **liquid**.

▲ Draw a box around each picture that shows a **location**.

▲ Draw a wavy line under each picture that shows a **symbol**.

▲ Draw straight line under each picture that shows a **country**.

▲ Draw an X over each picture that shows a **bird**.

▲ Draw a triangle around each picture that shows a **landmark**.

categories 54

cross out

Cut off the bottom of this page and give it to someone else. Have that person read each item to you as you cross out the pictures that are described until each picture is crossed out. See additional suggestions for using this page on page 56.

→ Cross out every:

1. building
2. type of transportation
3. appliance
4. food
5. item made of wood
6. container
7. liquid
8. reptile
9. piece of sports equipment
10. instrument
11. fuel
12. animal

categories 55

cross out

Cut off the bottom of this page and give it to someone else. Have that person read each item to you as you cross out the pictures that are described until each picture is crossed out. See additional suggestions for using this page on page 56.

➜ Cross out every:

1. plant
2. structure
3. fastener
4. organism
5. symbol
6. light source
7. natural resource
8. tool
9. form of communication
10. tiny object
11. nonliving thing
12. electrical device

101 Language Activities Copyright © 2004 LinguiSystems, Inc.

categories 56

grid activity

→ See the directions on page 56.

things you plug in	things you do in the morning	things you hang up	round objects	emotions
sports	shiny objects	jobs	things that run	things that are fast
weather words	things that fly	instruments	things that are quiet	zoo animals
farm animals	vegetables	fruits	tools	eating utensils
things made of plastic	things made of wood	things made of paper	types of pets	school supplies
communication devices	occupations	things you find in the bathroom	things with wheels	things that ring

101 Language Activities — Copyright © 2004 LinguiSystems, Inc.

categories

grid activity

→ See the directions on page 56.

ocean animals	sports	objects with wings	building materials	U.S. Presidents
buildings	valuable minerals	kitchen utensils	parts of speech	relatives
mammals	reptiles	units of measurement	pollutants	resources
internal organs	energy sources	settings	habitats	machines
liquids	famous inventors	school subjects	currency	seasons
holidays	months	farm animals	cities	disasters

categories 58

pie charts
→ See the instructions on page 56.

categories

☐ buildings ☐ North American countries
☐ famous inventions ☐ pollutants
☐ U.S. Presidents ☐ school subjects
☐ natural resources ☐ containers

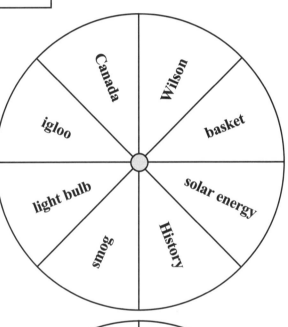
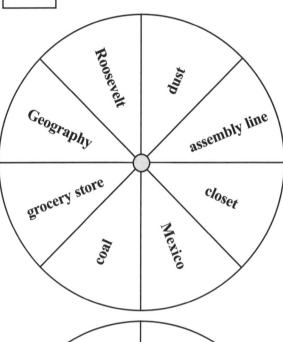
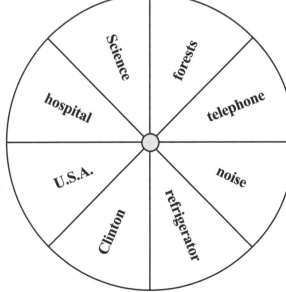

categories 59

pie charts
→ See the directions on page 56.

categories

☐ natural disasters   ☐ types of music

☐ U.S. states   ☐ emotions

☐ appliances   ☐ rivers

☐ beverages   ☐ clothing materials

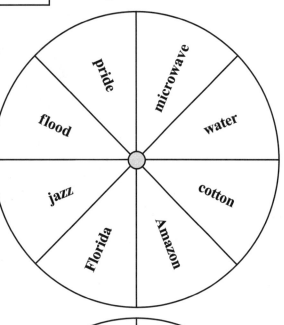
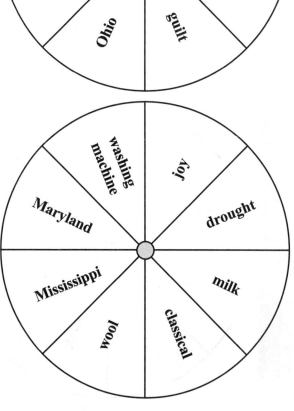

Wheel 1 (top-left): pride, microwave, water, cotton, Amazon, Florida, jazz, flood

Wheel 2 (top-right): coffee, denim, Nile, tornado, guilt, Ohio, stove, rock and roll

Wheel 3 (bottom-left): rap, refrigerator, Snake, leather, Oregon, earthquake, excitement, orange juice

Wheel 4 (bottom-right): washing machine, joy, drought, milk, classical, wool, Mississippi, Maryland

101 Language Activities   70   Copyright © 2004 LinguiSystems, Inc.

categories 60

pie charts
→ See the directions on page 56.

categories

☐ furniture ☐ punctuation
☐ oceans ☐ hobbies
☐ time words ☐ communication devices
☐ measurements ☐ relatives

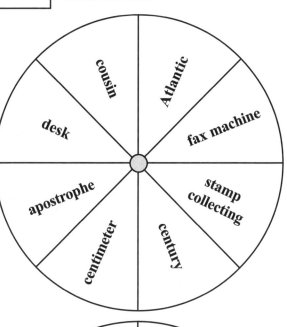

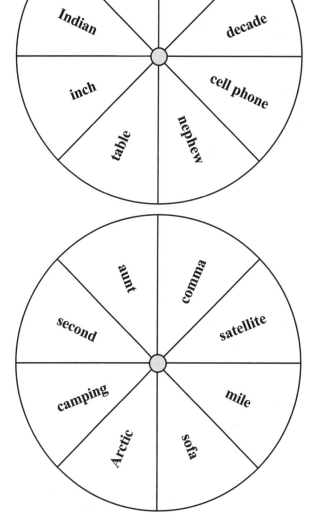

Comparisons – Introduction

Types of Activities

- **Describe It** (pages 73-75)
  Students will practice using the comparative forms of adjectives to make their language more precise and accurate.

- **Your Best Language** (pages 76-78)
  These activities challenge your students to choose similarities between items that are most significant in terms of comparison. For example, when comparing a fish and an octopus, it is more important to know that they are both ocean animals than that they both simply have eyes. That comparison would involve a larger set of possibilities. Encourage your students to choose the similarity that would narrow the comparison the most and exclude the most other possibilities.

- **Grid Activities** (pages 79-83)
  These pages can be used in a variety of ways. On the first four pages, students can randomly select an item on the grid and name a similarity that the two items listed have in common. You may also present the activity as a competitive game. Provide game tokens and a die, and then choose a direction for students to move around the grid (top to bottom, side to side). When a player lands on a pair of words on the grid, he names something the items have in common. The player writes his initials in the box on the grid. The game continues until all the boxes on the grid have been initialed. (As students roll the die and move, have them skip over boxes that have already been initialed.) The last grid activity (page 83) contains pairs of comparative/superlative adjectives scrambled around the board. Challenge students to match each pair of adjectives.

IEP Goals and Objectives:

- The student will identify correct use of age- and grade- appropriate comparatives and superlatives with 90% accuracy.
- The student will use comparatives and superlatives to modify curriculum-relevant vocabulary with 80% accuracy.
- The student will use age- and grade-level comparatives and superlatives in sentences with 80% accuracy.
- The student will compare and contrast age- and grade-level words with 80% accuracy.

Statements to Motivate

- You can describe things by telling how they are alike and different from other things.
- When you use comparative and superlative adjectives, your speaking and writing are much clearer. People will know exactly what you are talking about.
- Comparing words and their meanings helps your language become more accurate and specific.

comparisons 61

describe it

Adding the suffix *-er* to an adjective or the word *more* before it allows you to compare two things. Which of these two sentences tells you more information?

Our dog was dirty.
Our dog was dirt**ier** than the neighbor's dog.

→ Circle the word or words in each pair that would be used in a specific comparison:

1. wetter
   wet

2. more careful
   careful

3. nice
   nicer

4. interesting
   more interesting

→ Circle the sentence that is more specific:

5. The assignment was difficult
   The assignment was more difficult than the last one.

6. Her opinion was more correct than mine.
   Her opinion was correct, as was mine.

7. Visiting the dentist made him nervous.
   Visiting the dentist made him more nervous than visiting the doctor.

→ Fill in the blank with a suffix or word to make each comparison accurate.

8. My eyes are _____ sensitive without sunglasses.

9. Bill's business was _____ successful than Tom's.

10. You will make few_____ mistakes if you listen to directions.

11. I will be _____ prepared for the next test.

12. New York City is big_____ than Kansas City.

101 Language Activities

comparisons 62

describe it

Adding the suffix *-est* to an adjective or the word *most* before it allows you to compare many things. Which of these two sentences tells you more information?

Alaska is a cold state.
Alaska is the cold**est** state in the U.S.

→ Circle the word or words in each pair that would be used in a specific comparison:

1. sharp
   sharpest

2. sunniest
   sunny

3. interesting
   most interesting

4. most popular
   popular

→ Circle the sentence that is more specific:

5. That knife is dull.
   That is the dullest knife we own.

6. The movie was the most boring thing I've seen all year.
   The movie was boring.

7. Carrots are a healthy snack.
   Carrots are the healthiest snack I eat.

→ Fill in the blank with a suffix or word to make each comparison accurate.

8. Diamonds are one of the _____ precious gems.

9. Antarctica is the cold_____ continent.

10. Shaquille O'Neal was the _____ valuable player.

11. Mercury is the small_____ planet.

12. The world's old_____ plant is a 10,000-year-old bush in New England.

comparisons 63

describe it

Adding the suffix *-er* or *-est* to an adjective or the word *more* or *most* before it allows you to compare things

➜ Circle the word or words in each pair that would be used in a specific comparison:

1. bright
   brighter
2. lower
   low
3. most specific
   specific
4. more difficult
   difficult

➜ Circle the sentence that is more specific:

5. This is the slowest printer I have ever owned.
   This printer is very slow.

6. When it came to power, Superman had a lot.
   Superman was more powerful than a locomotive.

7. You used the best strategy of anyone.
   That was a good strategy you used.

8. The redwood is a tall tree.
   The redwood is the world's tallest tree.

➜ Fill in the blank with a suffix or word to make each comparison accurate.

9. Cars are _____ dangerous than airplanes.
10. I have the _____ difficult homework that I've ever had.
11. Their cat seems _____ playful than ours.
12. That calf is the small_____ cow that I've ever seen.
13. The orchestra played _____ beautifully today than it did last week.

comparisons 64

your best language

Some descriptions make a clearer comparison between items. Which of these is the most important similarity between *cameras* and *eyes*?

> They are objects.
> They focus.

There are thousands of "objects" in the world, but only a handful that focus. The second choice is more precise.

→ Circle the similarity that is most important for each pair of items.

1. fish — octopus	They have eyes.	They live in the ocean.
2. authors — composers	They are creative.	They are people.
3. 5/6 — 3/20	They are fractions.	They are numbers.
4. electrical wires — blood vessels	Something flows through them.	They are thin.
5. Saturday — Sunday	They are days of the week.	They are weekend days.
6. Moscow — London	They are cities.	They are capital cities.
7. where — when	They are question words.	They are words.
8. oxygen — nitrogen	They are gases.	They are in the air we breathe.
9. computer monitor — TV	They are machines.	They display information.
10. cup — suitcase	They are household items.	They have handles.

comparisons 65

your best language

Some descriptions make a clearer comparison between items. Which of these is the most important similarity between *blue* and *black*?

> They both start with the letter "b."
> They are both colors.

It doesn't really matter what letter the words start with because lots of things start with a "b." It's more important to know that these are both colors. The second similarity is more important and precise.

➔ Circle the similarity that is most important for each pair of items.

1. calculator — computer	They have buttons.	They are useful tools.
2. telescope — microscope	People use them.	They use lenses to magnify.
3. high school — college	People go there to learn.	They are in buildings.
4. length — width	You can see them.	They are measurements.
5. trumpet — saxophone	They are musical instruments.	They are shiny.
6. sphere — cylinder	They are round.	They are three-dimensional shapes.
7. Texas — Alaska	They are the largest U.S. states.	They are located in the U.S.
8. forest — ocean	They are places.	They are habitats.

101 Language Activities   Copyright © 2004 LinguiSystems, Inc.

comparisons 66

your best language

Some descriptions make a clearer comparison between items. Which of these is the most important characteristic of *pencils* and *pens*?

> Pens are made of metal or plastic.
> Pencil marks can be easily erased.

It doesn't really matter what material a pencil or pen is made of, because lots of things are made of metal or plastic. It's more important to know that pencil marks are erasable. The second characteristic is more important and precise.

➡ Circle the characteristic that is most important for each pair of items.

1. U.S. Constitution — book report | The Constitution has more words. | The Constitution is the foundation of a nation.

2. Earth — Jupiter | Jupiter is larger than Earth. | Earth can support life.

3. thermometer — scale | They are made of different materials. | They measure different things.

4. China — Los Angeles | They are different kinds of places. | China is a country, and Los Angeles is a city.

5. Benjamin Franklin — Albert Einstein | Only Einstein had a mustache | They both made important discoveries.

6. oceans — rivers | Rivers are narrower than oceans. | Oceans contain saltwater and rivers contain freshwater.

7. book — magazine | A magazine has more pictures. | A book gives you more detailed information.

8. spider — beetle | A spider has more legs. | A spider is an arachnid, not an insect.

grid activity—compare

→ See the directions on page 72.

owl/duck	Thomas Jefferson/ George Washington	oxygen/nitrogen	cameras/eyes
beige/purple	authors/ composers	English/Spanish	J.K. Rowling/ Roald Dahl
jazz/blues	Thanksgiving/ New Year's Day	electricity/fire	geometry/ algebra
clarinet/flute	Mexico City/ Washington, D.C.	Phoenix/ Sacramento	south/west
gold/iron	electrical wires/ blood vessels	decimals/ periods	CDs/books
cash/credit card	horse/motor	sun/oven	pulley/lever
Japan/China	skyscraper/ giraffe	Albert Einstein/ Benjamin Franklin	telephone/ cell phone

comparisons 68

grid activity–contrast

→ See the directions on page 72.

rat/squirrel	war/battle	thermometer/scale	comet/asteroid
parallel lines/perpendicular lines	whole number/fraction	noun/verb	map/globe
newspaper/magazine	fact/opinion	photograph/painting	conclusion/introduction
spider/cockroach	tree/bush	wall/ceiling	dictionary/encyclopedia
paper/plastic	elbow/knee	country/continent	ocean/lake
poison/antidote	turtle/tortoise	car/truck	canoe/yacht
scissors/knife	Ulysses S. Grant/Robert E. Lee	century/decade	thunderstorm/blizzard

comparisons 69

grid activity–compare & contrast

→ See the directions on page 72.

eagle/penguin	mountain/hill	crab/spider	lizard/crocodile
carrots/spinach	longitude/latitude	forest/desert	lungs/heart
lightning/thunder	test tube/window	sphere/cylinder	Hawaii/Australia
electron/proton	hurricane/tornado	length/width	snake/worm
Pennsylvania/Missouri	Montreal/Toronto	flat/steep	notebook/folder
deep/shallow	skeleton/skin	oxygen/nitrogen	sneeze/cough
microscope/telescope	vitamins/calories	stairs/elevator	calendar/clock

grid activity–compare & contrast

→ See the directions on page 72.

denominator/ numerator	bored/interested	Internet/TV	China/Brazil
history/ geography	test/homework	T-Rex/ brachiosaur	pillow/ marshmallow
(British) pound/ dollar	grapes/ potato chips	Pacific Ocean/ Atlantic Ocean	helmet/shield
speaker/ headphones	keyboard/guitar	sculpture/mobile	football/soccer
taco/burrito	helmet/knee pads	rice/noodles	orange juice/ milk
North Pole/ South Pole	Revolutionary War/Civil War	hotel/ campground	rain forest/tundra
dolphin/ killer whale	library/bookstore	ice cream/yogurt	tape measure/ ruler

comparisons

grid activity—compare

→ See the directions on page 72.

easier	most popular	more difficult	quicker
most appropriate	smaller	funniest	fewer
most difficult	quickest	easiest	louder
heaviest	more exciting	most expensive	more popular
straightest	smallest	most exciting	better
funnier	fewest	heavier	more appropriate
more expensive	best	straighter	loudest

Describing and Defining– Introduction

Types of Activities

- **Describe It** (pages 86-89)
  These activities challenge students to match descriptive phrases to specific items. Some of these phrases are intentionally ambiguous and will apply to more than one item. Encourage discussion and debate among students as they match items and descriptions.

- **Your Best Language** (pages 90-94)
  Students will begin to build definitions for items by providing adjectives and category names. Encourage students to be as specific as possible in the categories they select. For example, a cheetah is an *animal,* but it also belongs to other, more specific categories, including *wild animal, mammal, land animal, predator,* etc. The last activity in this section (page 94), has students practice selecting the most specific descriptive phrase from two choices.

- **Grid Activities** (pages 95-98)
  These pages can be used in a variety of ways. Students can randomly select an item on the grid and name an object that matches the descriptive word(s) or phrase(s) listed. You may also present the activity as a competitive game. Provide game tokens and a die, and then choose a direction for students to move around the grid (top to bottom, side to side). When a player lands on a space on the grid, he names an item that is described by the word(s) or phrase(s) listed. If correct, the player writes his initials in the box on the grid. The game continues until all the boxes on the grid have been initialed. (As students roll the die and move, have them skip over boxes that have already been initialed.)

- **Pie Charts** (pages 99-101)
  These pages challenge students to match various descriptive aspects (descriptive phrase, category, example from same category) on each pie chart to an item at the top of the page. You might have your students simply list the words at the top of the page on another sheet of paper and add a single item from each pie chart that describes the item. A more visual approach to the activity is to have students assign a different pattern (stripes, polka dots), color, or number to each item at the top of the page and mark the box with that designation. The student then uses the same pattern, color, or number to mark the section of each pie chart that goes with the item. Only one section of each chart goes with the item. An example of a completed pie chart for a similar activity is shown on page 31.

IEP Goals and Objectives:
- The student will label curriculum vocabulary words given definitions with 90% accuracy.
- The student will use adjectives, categories, and examples to define age- and grade-level words with 80% accuracy.
- The student will use descriptive phrases to describe and define curriculum-relevant words with 80% accuracy.
- The student will use specific language when describing and defining curriculum content vocabulary with 80% accuracy.

Statements to Motivate
- Naming a word from its meaning is an important skill. It helps you find exactly the right word when you are speaking and writing.
- Good descriptions include examples, adjectives, and categories used in descriptive phrases and sentences.

describing & defining

describe it

You can use phrases to accurately describe things.

▲ Circle all the phrases that can describe a **courthouse**.

▲ Underline all the phrases that can describe a **sentence**.

▲ Put a box around all the phrases that can describe a **reptile**.

▲ Cross out all the phrases that can describe a **tusk**.

Note: You should mark all the phrases at least once. Some phrases may be marked more than once.

an important building	includes a noun and a verb	protrudes from a walrus' mouth
a location	cold-blooded	includes lizards and tortoises
requires order	protrudes from an elephant's mouth	have rough exteriors
rules are enforced	where a judge works	first letter capitalized
where juries do work	punctuation is necessary	made up of cells

describing & defining 73

describe it

You can use phrases to accurately describe things.

▲ Circle all the phrases that can describe a **tank**.

▲ Underline all the phrases that can describe the **U.S. Constitution**.

▲ Put a box around all the phrases that can describe **saliva**.

▲ Cross out all the phrases that can describe a **taste bud**.

Note: You should mark all the phrases at least once. Some phrases may be marked more than once.

is a liquid	ensures freedom	establishes rules for government
an important document	part of a car	written after the American Revolution
located on the surface of the tongue	makes chewing and swallowing easier	a type of container
can hold liquids and gases	transmits sensations to the brain	helps us experience sweet and sour
found in the mouth	consists of cells	might contain gasoline

101 Language Activities

describing & defining | 74

describe it

You can use phrases to accurately describe things.

▲ Circle all the phrases that can describe **dialogue**.

▲ Underline all the phrases that can describe an **organism**.

▲ Put a box around all the phrases that can describe **soil**.

▲ Cross out all the phrases that can describe a **prediction**.

Note: You should mark all the phrases at least once. Some phrases may be marked more than once.

an educated guess	written with quotation marks	can grow
made up of cells	assists understanding	may be correct or incorrect
can be deep	requires support	a type of habitat
a look into the future	often has layers	has minerals and decomposing matter
a type of communication	may be friendly or unfriendly	can be big or small

101 Language Activities

describing & defining 75

describe it

You can use phrases to accurately describe things.

▲ Circle all the phrases that can describe **solar energy**.

▲ Underline all the phrases that can describe **Russia**.

▲ Put a box around all the phrases that can describe a **parasite**.

▲ Cross out all the phrases that can describe an **anthill**.

Note: You should mark all the phrases at least once. Some phrases may be marked more than once.

has a large population	best to be avoided	produces little pollution
can be warm	can be part of an infestation	part of former Soviet Union
lives inside a host	large country	often cone-shaped
may cause destruction	a type of nest	may live inside intestines
a lot of activity goes on inside it	requires the sun	most abundant energy on Earth

101 Language Activities   Copyright © 2004 LinguiSystems, Inc.

describing & defining 76

your best language

A good definition might include adjectives and the category an item belongs to. Use an adjective and a category name to describe each item. The first one is done for you.

item	adjective	category
1. cheetah	*fast*	*mammal*
2. corn		
3. pizza		
4. summer		
5. happiness		
6. Europe		
7. Alaska		
8. space shuttle		
9. banana		
10. ice cream		
11. July		
12. volcano		
13. 1/20		
14. Tyrannosaurus Rex		
15. computer		

describing & defining 77

your best language

A good definition might include adjectives and the category an item belongs to. Use an adjective and a category name to describe each item.

item	adjective	category
1. cancer		
2. redwood		
3. Antarctica		
4. Columbus		
5. a		
6. neutron		
7. cake		
8. gold		
9. Seattle		
10. coffee		
11. truck		
12. guitar		
13. football		
14. Asia		
15. light bulb		

describing & defining — 78

your best language

A good definition might include adjectives and the category an item belongs to. Use two adjectives and a category name to describe each item. The first one is done for you.

item	adjective	adjective	category
1. elephant	huge	gray	land animal
2. hospital			
3. flute			
4. glacier			
5. aspirin			
6. gravity			
7. bacteria			
8. morning			
9. college			
10. uniform			
11. poster			
12. calculator			
13. hammer			
14. blizzard			
15. amusement park			

describing & defining

your best language

A good definition might include adjectives and the category an item belongs to. Use two adjectives and a category name to describe each item.

item	adjective	adjective	category
1. factory			
2. violet			
3. hurricane			
4. adjective			
5. iron			
6. December			
7. refrigerator			
8. paper			
9. kickball			
10. bicycle			
11. lunch			
12. essay			
13. fire			
14. couch			
15. lemonade			

101 Language Activities

describing & defining | 80

your best language

It's best to use the most specific words when describing something. Circle the phrase that most accurately describes each item. The first one is done for you.

item	descriptive phrases	
1. ostrich	has feathers	(a flightless bird)
2. noun	a word	person, place, or thing
3. solid	something you can feel	state of matter that is not liquid or gas
4. Washington, D.C.	important city	capital of the U.S.A.
5. triceratops	large, extinct animal	three-horned dinosaur
6. praying mantis	green animal	long-legged insect
7. cola	cold beverage	brown soda
8. freedom	good feeling	liberty and independence
9. election	annual event	a vote to choose leaders
10. rock and roll	loud, energetic music	type of song
11. sweatshirt	long-sleeved clothing	warm, heavy type of shirt
12. snake	long, thin animal	legless reptile
13. Internet	informational resource	place to look up stuff
14. 3	small prime number	number after 2
15. soccer	activity that uses a ball	world's most popular sport

describing & defining | 81

grid activity

→ See the directions on page 84.

can contract part of the body example: biceps	insect round and hard-shelled black and red	substance metal used to make pennies and pipes	kitchen utensil sharp used for cutting steak
music-making device played by humans example: piano	force causes objects to attract affects metals	appliance small and rectangular cooks food quickly	beverage often hot often drank in the morning
noise can be soft or loud made by a bird	body of water flows between banks example: Nile	building public place treats sick and injured people	leader Chief Executive of the United States example: George Bush
person family member example: aunt	large land area continent contains France and Italy	natural resource fossil fuel used in cars	force causes objects to attract affects metals
piece of writing has ingredients and directions used in cooking	vacation spot sand and waves next to the ocean	body of water found in the Eastern Hemisphere borders India and Africa	annual event determines leaders has campaigns and ballots

describing & defining | 82

grid activity

→ See the directions on page 84.

located above the Earth protective layer of air	international competition held every four years	where a species lives example: ocean	where large populations live example: Miami
electrical device used to amplify the voice	building contains dozens of floors	space object orbits the Earth	lightweight appendage helps birds fly
a grain used to make bread	healthy food examples: celery, carrots	bendable body part found between calf and thigh	space objects chunks of rock and ice
famous invention voice communication device	rock indentations ancient markings of life	large area contains saltwater	relationship between nations not a hostile situation
national symbols designs on cloth	scientific occupation performs experiments and gathers data	area of land totally surrounded by water	measure of time 365 days

describing & defining 83

grid activity

→ See the directions on page 84.

makes a good pet	bird that quacks	something that glows	large area of grassy land	national capital city
to spend foolishly	correct	noise a dog makes	direction	sound a bell makes
condition that causes sneezing	simple; not fancy	to bend down	place to store things	piece of jewelry
small wound	something to hold soup	part of stairs	courtroom occupation	measuring tool
moving water	place for dirty dishes	garbage	walking motion	time of year
gesture of greeting	used to improve taste of food	has a handle	floats easily	stores information

describing & defining | 84

grid activity

→ See the directions on page 84.

to lift something	to hang	to run a short distance at top speed	greeting motion with hand	thick wire or cord
measures inches and centimeters	to hit with a hammer	TV service	tropical location	cold location
place for dogs	leader of a nation	punctuation mark	mathematical symbol	something you do before a test
dry cake ingredient	someone who looks after children	leaves a stain on clothing	important medical occupation	to take something that isn't yours
to make something new	requires training and skill	vigorous activity	gift-giving occasion	pack animal
strong negative feeling	person who deserves respect	person who is not well-liked	place people go to relax	someone who watches an event

describing & defining 85

pie charts
→ See the directions on page 84.

words

☐ movie
☐ quartz
☐ box
☐ tennis
☐ water
☐ Asia
☐ aphid
☐ tropical

Description

(pie chart segments: located in Western Hemisphere, clear and tasteless, shown on a large screen, usually made of cardboard, warm year-round, played on a large court, damages house plants, used to make glass)

Category

(pie chart segments: insect, storage container, continent, mineral, racquet sport, form of entertainment, liquid, climate)

Example from Same Category

(pie chart segments: ladybug, milk, polar, badminton, Europe, mica, TV, cabinet)

101 Language Activities — 99 — Copyright © 2004 LinguiSystems, Inc.

describing & defining | 86

pie charts
→ See the directions on page 84.

words

☐ microscope
☐ medal
☐ hyena
☐ hurricane
☐ barometric pressure
☐ subway
☐ book
☐ space shuttle

Description

(underground train; lets you see tiny objects; piece of metal on a ribbon; contains a long story; measurement of air pressure; lives on African savannah; reusable Earth orbiter; high winds and surf)

Category

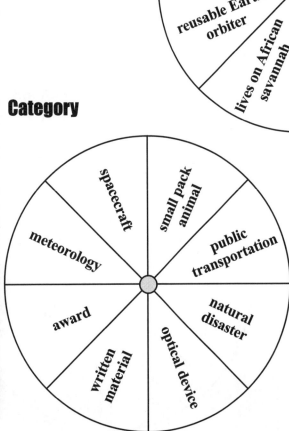
(spacecraft; small pack animal; public transportation; natural disaster; optical device; written material; award; meteorology)

Example from Same Category

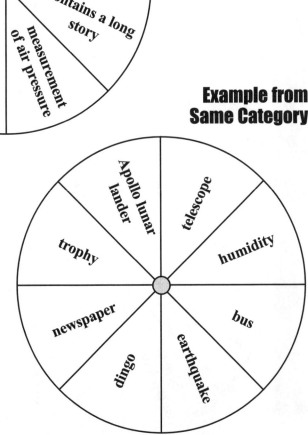
(Apollo lunar lander; telescope; humidity; bus; earthquake; dingo; newspaper; trophy)

describing & defining 87

pie charts
→ See the directions on page 84.

words

☐ quotation mark ☐ vision
☐ lever ☐ Civil War
☐ Alice ☐ Eric the Red
☐ adjective ☐ judicial

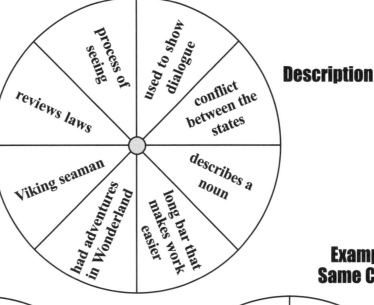

Description

- process of seeing
- used to show dialogue
- conflict between the states
- describes a noun
- long bar that makes work easier
- had adventures in Wonderland
- Viking seaman
- reviews laws

Category

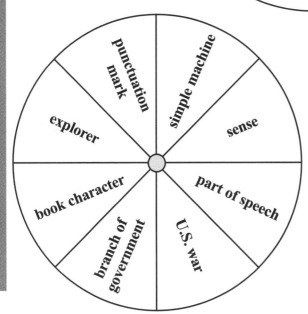

- punctuation mark
- simple machine
- sense
- part of speech
- U.S. war
- branch of government
- book character
- explorer

Example from Same Category

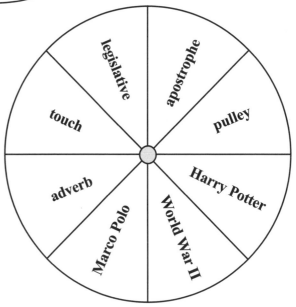

- legislative
- apostrophe
- pulley
- Harry Potter
- World War II
- Marco Polo
- adverb
- touch

101 Language Activities **101** Copyright © 2004 LinguiSystems, Inc.

Paraphrasing – Introduction

Types of Activities

- **Say It Again** (pages 103-108)
  These activities introduce your students to the concept of paraphrasing. Students match sentences with ones that have been paraphrased using synonyms or alternate phrasing. On the last two pages (107-108), students are challenged to provide alternate words to complete a paraphrased sentence.

- **Your Best Language** (pages 109-114)
  Various aspects of paraphrasing are addressed in these activities, including using specific language to retain or enhance meaning. Students will practice paraphrasing their own sentences on the last three pages (112-114).

- **Grid Activities** (pages 115-116)
  These pages can be used in a variety of ways. Students can randomly select a sentence on the grid and paraphrase it. You may also present the activity as a competitive game. Provide game tokens and a die, and then choose a direction for students to move around the grid (top to bottom, side to side). When a player lands on a grid space, she paraphrases that sentence. If correct, the player writes her initials in the box on the grid. The game continues until all the boxes on the grid have been initialed. (As students roll the die and move, have them skip over boxes that have already been initialed.)

IEP Goals and Objectives:

- The student will identify correct paraphrasing of sentences/paragraphs with 90% accuracy.
- The student will accurately provide paraphrasing of sentences and paragraphs that include curriculum content with 80% accuracy.
- The student will describe how paraphrasing increases understanding of classroom information with 90% accuracy.

Statements to Motivate

- Paraphrasing is a good way to practice using synonyms.
- Paraphrasing shows teachers that you understand what you just read or heard.
- Paraphrasing helps you understand what you just read or heard. If you can repeat information accurately in your own words, you will understand it and remember it better and longer.

paraphrasing 88

say it again

When you paraphrase something, you say the same information in a different way.

→ Read each sentence on the left. Draw a line to the sentence on the right that paraphrases it.

1. The mouse picked up the cheese and ate it.

2. A capital is where government leaders meet.

3. George saw the tree being chopped down.

4. Microscopes magnify images.

5. Reptiles' scaly skin helps to hold in moisture.

6. Six-legged bugs have compound visual sensors.

7. I can't see very well without my glasses.

8. Mold is in the same plant family as mushrooms.

a. A capital is a meeting place for government leaders.

b. George watched as the tree was chopped down.

c. Insects see with many eyes.

d. Mushrooms are related to mold.

e. My glasses help me see.

f. The mouse ate the cheese that he picked up.

g. The skin of reptiles helps to keep moisture inside them.

h. You can see images in great detail with microscopes.

101 Language Activities   Copyright © 2004 LinguiSystems, Inc.

paraphrasing 89

say it again

When you paraphrase something, you say the same information in a different way.

→ Read each sentence on the left. Draw a line to the sentence on the right that paraphrases it.

1. One type of container is a jar.

2. Fossils occur when bones turn into stone.

3. The country that is north of the United States has has cold winters.

4. I took the bus home from school.

5. Mickey Mouse has very small arms.

6. How is it going?

7. He was locked out of his house.

8. The first humans like us lived about 30,000 years ago.

a. Because he forgot his key, he couldn't get into his house.

b. Bones turning into stone create fossils.

c. Canada has cold winters.

d. How are you doing?

e. I got home by taking the bus.

f. Jars are one type of container.

g. Modern humans have been around for about 30,000 years.

h. The arms on Mickey Mouse are tiny.

paraphrasing 90

say it again

Paraphrasing may involve changing around words or using synonyms.

➔ Read each sentence on the left. Draw a line to the sentence on the right that paraphrases it.

1. You are right.   a. My temperature is fine.

2. My temperature is normal.   b. The calculator is defective.

3. The calculator is broken.   c. The clown is humorous.

4. The feather's weight was not heavy.   d. The feather was light.

5. The clown is funny.   e. The tree bark feels rough.

6. The tree bark does not feel smooth.   f. The whole meal was delicious.

7. The entire meal was tasty.   g. Turtles can be shy.

8. Turtles can be easily frightened.   h. You are correct.

paraphrasing 91

say it again

Paraphrasing may involve changing around words or using synonyms.

➜ Read each sentence on the left. Draw a line to the sentence on the right that paraphrases it.

1. The words are out of order

2. Three apples are less than five apples.

3. Draw a box around the word.

4. You're supposed to mix the ingredients.

5. Of the holidays, I like Christmas the best.

6. Where are you?

7. The police officer investigated the crime.

8. Capitalize the first letter of a name.

a. Christmas is my favorite holiday.

b. Draw a square around the word.

c. Make the first letter of a name in uppercase.

d. The ingredients need to be mixed.

e. The police officer checked out the crime.

f. The sentence has incorrect sequence.

g. Three apples are not as many as five apples.

h. What is your location?

paraphrasing 92

say it again

→ Complete each incomplete sentence by paraphrasing the information in the first sentence.

1. Her birthday is the day after Thursday.

   Her birthday is _____.

2. You can see images in great detail with microscopes.

   Microscopes _____ images.

3. Actors must know their lines by heart.

   Actors must _____ their lines.

4. One half of the kids in our class are girls.

   Fifty _____ of the kids in our class are girls.

5. Twenty-three minus ten equals thirteen.

   If you _____ ten from twenty-three, you get thirteen.

6. The thing that you throw trash into tipped over.

   The _____ tipped over.

7. My meeting begins halfway between 8:00 and 9:00.

   My meeting is at _____.

8. Melted ice was all over the sidewalk.

   Melted ice was _____ the sidewalk.

9. I don't really enjoy extremely high temperatures.

   I don't really enjoy _____ weather.

10. Every sentence must have an action or being word and a noun.

    Every sentence must have a _____ and a noun.

101 Language Activities Copyright © 2004 LinguiSystems, Inc.

paraphrasing 93

say it again

→ Complete each incomplete sentence by paraphrasing the information in the first sentence.

1. My room was spotless after I picked it up.

    After picking up my room, it was _____.

2. The Colorado River has many curves.

    The Colorado River has many _____.

3. The seven dwarves liked to whistle while they earned a living.

    The seven dwarves like to whistle while they _____.

4. That old dog is the opposite of energetic.

    That old dog is _____.

5. When people are sick, doctors may prescribe medicine.

    Doctors sometimes prescribe medicine to fight _____.

6. Strong earthquakes can cause many things to break or crumble.

    Strong earthquakes can cause a lot of _____.

7. Trees do not produce cash.

    _____ does not grow on trees.

8. Rainbows have seven different shades of light.

    Rainbows have seven different _____.

9. My mom's mom is retired.

    My _____ no longer works.

10. I need to review the material the night before the exam.

    I need to _____ the night before the test.

paraphrasing 94

your best language

One reason to paraphrase is to make your language more specific.

→ Circle the sentence that contains the most specific information in each pair.

1. The Earth's atmosphere has many layers.

    The atmosphere has many parts.

2. Colin was stung by the insect.

    Colin was stung by a wasp.

3. Throw that thing away!

    Throw that smelly banana peel away!

4. Gutenberg invented the printing press around 1450.

    The guy who invented the printing press did so in the fifteenth century.

5. They don't like the music that uses a lot of instruments.

    They don't like classical music.

6. That guy was a great speaker.

    Martin Luther King, Jr., was a great speaker.

7. He selected *The Adventures of Huckleberry Finn* for his book report.

    He will do his book report on a novel about an American boy.

8. Don moved here from a state with palm trees.

    Don moved here from Hawaii.

9. Jeanine used a powerful tool to research her report.

    Jeanine researched her report using the Internet.

paraphrasing | **95**

your best language

One reason to paraphrase is to make your language more specific.

→ Circle the sentence that contains the most specific information in each pair.

1. The ambulance took her there yesterday.
   The ambulance took her to the hospital yesterday.

2. My birthday is January ninth.
   My birthday will be in a few months.

3. According to the thermometer, this is one of the hottest days of the year.
   According to the thing that measures temperature, it is 100 degrees.

4. Dinosaurs have been extinct for millions of years.
   Dinosaurs have not roamed the earth for a long time.

5. World War II was over by 1946.
   World War II ended in 1945.

6. That sentence is missing something.
   That sentence needs a comma between the clauses.

7. Our teacher gave us a huge assignment for the weekend.
   We have to write a ten-page research report by Monday.

8. There are substances that can cause great harm to the environment.
   Both oil and mercury can harm the environment.

paraphrasing 96

your best language

One reason to paraphrase is to make your language more specific.

→ Circle the sentence that contains the most specific information in each pair.

1. The Civil War divided the United States during the 1860s.

    There was conflict in the United States during the 1860s.

2. Palm trees do not grow well in all climates.

    Palm trees only grow in warm, tropical climates.

3. The hot air balloon passed over our neighborhood.

    The hot air balloon went right over our house.

4. One large land mass on Earth is uninhabited.

    No one permanently lives in Antarctica.

5. You will lose five points for not signing your paper.

    If you do not sign your paper, you will not get full credit.

6. There is a force that causes some objects to be attracted to one another.

    Magnetism causes some objects to be attracted to one another.

7. Whales may not be the largest animals in the oceans.

    Giant squids may be the largest ocean animals.

8. Our teacher gave us time to complete the test.

    We had one hour to finish the test.

paraphrasing 97

your best language

→ Paraphrase each sentence without using the italicized word(s). You may change other words, too, as long as the meaning stays the same.

1. I sure could use some *assistance* with this project.

2. *Palm trees* can produce dates and coconuts.

3. The *airplane* flew over our building.

4. There are seven *continents* on Earth.

5. My dog needs to go to the *veterinarian* to receive treatment for a *parasite*.

6. The *Civil War* divided the United States during the 1860s.

7. She asked me to *pass* the *container* of tissue.

8. The calendar will have to be thrown away on *the last day of December*.

9. A lot of people wanted George Washington to be a *royal leader* instead of a president.

10. The *anxious* kid was at the *start* of the line.

paraphrasing 98

your best language

→ Paraphrase each sentence. You may change words, use synonyms, or completely reword the sentence, as long as the meaning stays the same. Use specific language! An example is done for you.

1. Antarctica is a cold place.
   Antarctica is a very icy continent.

2. Germany is next to France.

3. For a long time, people used to think the world was flat.

4. When you wipe your hair on a balloon, it stands up because of static electricity.

5. Leaders of our world have long struggled to achieve peace.

6. The moon orbits the Earth.

7. According to the thermometer, it was well below freezing last night.

8. The police had proof that the man committed the crime.

9. Vegetables are good for you.

10. My sister estimated that her yearly allowance will be one thousand dollars.

paraphrasing 99

your best language

→ Paraphrase each sentence. You may change words, use synonyms, or completely reword the sentence, as long as the meaning stays the same. Use specific language! An example is done for you.

1. Carlos was bitten by the animal.
   The dog bit Carlos in the leg.

2. They don't like loud, noisy music.

3. Margaret moved here from Texas.

4. She selected *Harriet the Spy* for her book report.

5. Everything is composed of atoms.

6. The assembly line helped to make factories more productive.

7. Her bumping into the tree trunk was an event that could not be avoided.

8. After building the new neighborhood center, everyone wanted to express their gratitude to the millionaire.

9. You can't have dessert until you've finished your meatloaf.

10. Except for the teacher, the room was vacant.

paraphrasing 100

grid activity

→ See the directions on page 102.

I need assistance.	She completed the work she took home today.	The sun was glowing with a lot of light today.	There are many large chunks of rock and ice with tails in space.
The announcer used the object that amplifies her voice.	The teacher's answer was not correct.	The dog was making a lot of noise.	The scientists uncovered an ancient record of life made of bone.
Hal was not at school today.	I picked up the receiver and pushed some buttons.	I finished before anyone else.	My stomach feels empty.
I pushed the button so the TV would come on.	My mom picked up the bag of trash, closed it, and carried it to the curb.	The back and forth motion of the chair helped the baby go to sleep.	The cat was not well-behaved while we were away.
He put his hand to his forehead when he said the Pledge of Allegiance.	I was feeling ready for bed.	The judge had an angry look on his face.	At 6:00, she began her morning routine.
The moon travels in a circular path around the Earth.	I know it is not good for my health to stay idle all the time.	Einstein was a man who had a lot of information.	My dad lifted the dishes before scrubbing and rinsing them.

paraphrasing 101

grid activity

→ See the directions on page 102.

We looked at the words in the book and comprehended them.	I need to take that book from the library and leave after giving them my card.	In a few weeks I will go back to the library and give them back the book.	Every Sunday afternoon we eat lunch outside our home.
The speech was not interesting.	Chimpanzees use their arms to move around in trees.	Take away six from fifteen and you get nine.	Tammy ate 50% of that fruit pie.
There were five problems that were done incorrectly.	The day before today was Mary's birthday.	Paleontologists study animals that no longer live on Earth.	Have me remember that again later.
Alaska is by no means the smallest state in the U.S.	The doctor took some internal pictures of my hand.	We really had an enjoyable time with our friends last night.	In order to return an item, you need proof of its purchase.
If you would like to dine here tonight, you must call ahead of time.	Can you pick up some food items for me when you come home?	She is in front of the TV all the time.	She did not care for the sweater she received.

Answer Key

page 7
Student answers will vary.
Following are suggested answers:
story character: short, imaginary, smelly, dangerous, mysterious, helpful, tall
gasoline: liquid, smelly, dangerous, expensive
plot of a story: imaginary, confusing, mysterious, scary, long
homework assignment: short, easy, confusing, difficult, educational, long

page 8
Student answers will vary.
Following are suggested answers:
explorer: tired, strong, weak, sick, brilliant, intelligent, brave, busy, unhealthy, curious, interesting
patient in a hospital: tired, weak, sick, unhealthy
political candidate: tired, strong, weak, brilliant, intelligent, brave, busy, curious, interesting, tricky
piece of candy: sweet, sticky, gooey

page 9
There may be other combinations that work besides the ones given, but these seem the most likely.
story character: imaginary, tricky
story plot: mysterious, scary
gasoline: smelly, expensive
homework assignment: educational, difficult
explorer: curious, brave
hospital patient: unhealthy, weak
political candidate: busy, intelligent

page 10
Student answers will vary.
Following are suggested answers:
1. black, sticky
2. wooden, stringed
3. large, busy
4. loud, entertaining
5. radioactive, rare
6. quick, automatic
7. long, narrow
8. complicated, expensive
9. fast, exciting
10. hard, shiny

page 11
Student answers will vary.
Following are suggested answers:
1. cold, icy
2. hard, floating
3. rectangular, national
4. green, crunchy
5. hard, thin
6. long, wild
7. national, fall
8. thin, white
9. important, communication
10. thin, bendable

page 12
1. alive, organism
2. historic, event
3. alert, listener
4. microscopic, cell
5. level, parking lot
6. powerful, computer
7. curved, apostrophe
8. popular, song

page 13
1. bumpy, road
2. nervous, performer
3. meaningful, word
4. straight, line
5. amazing, discovery
6. fiery, eruption
7. tropical, region
8. natural, resource

page 14
There may be other combinations that work besides the ones given, but these seem the most likely.
1. **politician:** popular, trustworthy
2. **motorcycle:** expensive, dangerous
3. **mountain:** volcanic, massive
4. **window:** tinted, transparent
5. **story:** imaginary, creative
6. **chart:** informative, organized
7. **ruler:** straight, precise
8. **nation:** foreign, huge

page 15
There may be other combinations that work besides the ones given, but these seem the most likely.
1. **citizen:** concerned, responsible
2. **disease:** unknown, tragic
3. **emergency:** medical, urgent
4. **island:** tropical, isolated
5. **surgeon:** competent, skillful
6. **library:** quiet, educational
7. **egg:** fragile, cracked
8. **cabinet:** locked, wooden
9. **gasoline:** expensive, explosive

page 19
These words should be underlined in each sentence:
1. conclusion
2. estimate
3. solution
4. belief
5. more
6. disappear
7. community
8. location
9. creator
10. mistake

Answers will vary on pages not listed.

Answer Key

page 20

These words should be underlined in each sentence:

1. lengthy
2. correct
3. high
4. nearest
5. huge
6. fast
7. blunt
8. appropriate
9. profitable
10. nervous

page 21

The word listed first should be underlined. The second word should be written in the blank.

1. saved, rescued
2. under, below
3. vacant, empty
4. error, mistake
5. writer, author
6. present, gift
7. gentle, careful
8. clean, spotless
9. information, evidence
10. strategy, plan

page 22

The word listed first should be underlined. The second word should be written in the blank.

1. many, several
2. whole, entire
3. joined, together
4. crooked, bent
5. old, ancient
6. sheet, paper
7. countries, nations
8. smart, intelligent
9. clear, obvious
10. access, entrance

page 23

vacant, empty
beneath, below
saved, rescued
crooked, bent
little, small
furious, angry
vanish, disappear
container, holder
exchange, trade
liberty, freedom
wealthy, rich
present, gift
nation, country
reply, answer
writer, author
hide conceal
error, mistake
spotless, clean
smart, intelligent
pick, choose

page 24

broken, fixed
cloudy, sunny
reward, punish
energetic, lazy
outside, inside
arrive, leave
bumpy, flat
first, last
safe, dangerous
interesting, boring
light, dark
open, close
rough, smooth
avoid, seek
new, ancient
subtract, add
friend, enemy
build, destroy
more, less

page 26

1. usual, common
2. sort, organize
3. predict, guess
4. feature, trait
5. ability, skill
6. appropriate, correct
7. flow, circulate
8. describe, explain

page 27

1. identify, recognize
2. job, occupation
3. custom, tradition
4. free, liberate
5. physician, doctor
6. freedom, independence
7. consider, regard
8. assertion, statement

page 28

1. east, west
2. past, future
3. nutritious, unhealthy
4. enter, exit
5. ceiling, floor
6. introduction, conclusion
7. denominator, numerator
8. crooked, straight

page 29

1. rough, smooth
2. ignore, listen
3. provide, receive
4. sweltering, frigid
5. best, worst
6. negative, positive
7. accidental, intentional
8. microscopic, massive

page 32

Student answers will vary. Following are suggested answers:

U.S. Constitution: rights, paragraph, vision, amendment, freedom, nation

Answers will vary on pages not listed.

Answer Key

North America: valley, problems, oil, freedom, nation

revised: report, paragraph, opinion, proposal, story, fact, amendment

confirmed: report, features, opinion, fact

page 33
Student answers will vary. Following are suggested answers:

cycle: election, energy, season, year, life, weather, erosion

organized: election, campaign, debate, government, research

Earth's crust: soil, copper, uranium, life, erosion

politics: election, campaign, promise, debate, government

page 34
Student answers will vary. Following are suggested answers:

paragraph: describe, define, communicate, explain

scientist: apply, communicate, observe, experiment, explain, learn, investigate

planet: pull, attract, repel, revolve, rotate, spin

magnet: pull, attract, repel

page 35
Student answers will vary. Following are suggested answers:

river: erode, saturate, flow, overflow

muscle: relax, flex, contract, blink

chart: compare, persuade, interpret, organize

judge: react, decide, question

page 36
Student answers will vary. Following are suggested answers:

industrial: factory, power lines, nuclear plant

focus: telescope, student, eye, binoculars

base: telescope, globe, battleship, Statue of Liberty, baseball diamond

store: box, battery, locker, computer, nuclear plant

current: power lines, battery, computer, outlet, nuclear plant

page 37
Student answers will vary. Following are suggested answers:

healthy: strawberry, running, apple, broccoli

politics: voting, U.S. Capitol

energy: sun, volcano, thunderstorm, battery, nuclear plant

light: feather, strawberry, violin, box, apple, battery, leaf, broccoli

open: door, box

page 38
1. computer, encyclopedia
2. violin, piano
3. Saturn, hand
4. sculpture, painting
5. student, light bulb
6. mouth, bus
7. baby, table
8. flower, cherry
9. rainbow, sunset
10. mesa, table

page 39
1. pencil, brain
2. vase, bone
3. mouth, telephone
4. map, compass
5. steak, gum
6. helmet, umbrella
7. credit card, check
8. tomatoes, trees

9. bleach, detergent
10. towel, deodorant

page 50
14	2	16	20
8	9	19	4
6	18	1	10
7	15	12	3
17	11	13	5

page 52
weather: unpredictable, occurs in cycles, affected by atmosphere, produces clouds

Earth's crust: outer layer, relatively thin, made of rocks and soil, where we live

saltwater: found in the ocean, undrinkable, liquid, home to large mammals

energy: released by the sun, valuable, generated by natural resources, needed for movement

plant cell: has a nucleus, where photosynthesis occurs, surrounded by a wall, alive

Great Depression: took place in 1930s, economic disaster, caused unemployment, lasted a decade

Civil War: deadly conflict, fight between states, took place in 1860s, lasted half a decade

dialogue: requires more than one person, explores thoughts and ideas, can be entertaining, back and forth

page 53
echoes: sound waves, bounces, heard in cliffs and valleys, used by bats

recycling: combats pollution, helps the environment, can be done with plastic, can be done with paper

Answers will vary on pages not listed.

Answer Key

the Universe: vast, expanding, mostly unexplored, contains galaxies
fossils: remains of ancient life, records in rock, helps archaeologists, often buried
Gandhi: unelected leader, protester, Indian, inspires leaders today
Europe: continent, contains many nations, has some Spanish speakers, neighbor of Asia
industry: needs raw materials, produces products, economic activity, may cause pollution
Mexico: North American nation, U.S. neighbor, has mostly Spanish speakers, warm climate

page 54
the brain: thinks, integrates information, made of nerve cells, learns
language: used to communicate, uses symbols, relies on words, can be colorful
atom: tiny, has a nucleus, is part of a molecule, has electrons and protons
election: uses ballots, part of a democracy, November event, part of political process
Jupiter: massive, gaseous, has a Great Red Spot, largest planet
population: group of something, can be diverse, number of people in a place, can vary over time
newspaper: contains journalism, needs advertisers, created by editors and reporters, needs subscribers
magnetism: a force, causes things to attract, has fields, is concerned with poles

page 55
freedom: guaranteed by the U.S. Constitution, not enjoyed by everyone, must be defended, important to democracy
President of the U.S.: chief executive, elected every four years, must be a U.S. citizen, can only serve two terms
history: in the past, something to learn from, record of events, story of people and events
business: economic activity, needs investors, consumers and producers, requires planning and organization
Internet: includes e-mail and web, uses computers, contains lots of information, links people all over the world
geometry: relationship between shapes, includes angles, includes planes and slopes, branch of mathematics
vocabulary: words you know, learned language, can be improved with work, contains antonyms and synonyms
media: influential group, reports news, comments on events, relies on advertisers

page 58
1. Canada
2. milk
3. Thomas Edison
4. adjective
5. couch
6. spring
7. cheerful
8. one dollar
9. Disneyland
10. chips

page 59
1. George Bush
2. gasoline
3. skyscraper
4. sugar
5. flute
6. tennis
7. verb
8. Florida
9. toast
10. amoeba

page 60
1. food
2. school supply
3. liquid
4. person
5. money
6. U.S.A.
7. word
8. shape
9. metal
10. city

page 61
1. furniture
2. appliance
3. clothing
4. character
5. time of year
6. math
7. vehicle
8. meat
9. instrument
10. device

page 62
1. part of speech
2. individual
3. bedroom
4. pilot
5. healthy
6. unhealthy
7. Europe
8. February
9. small
10. unhappy

Answers will vary on pages not listed.

Answer Key

page 63
animal: zebra, elephant, ant, fish, duck
container: popcorn, chemical tank, balloon, chips, basket, sunscreen, ketchup, box, gift, hair spray
healthy food: popcorn, grapes, fish, apple
unhealthy: cigarette, factory, chemical tank, chips, candy bar
chemical: cigarette, factory, chemical tank, sunscreen, hair spray
snack: popcorn, grapes, chips, apple, candy bar

page 64
liquid: glass of water, soda, bird bath
location: Hawaii, Egypt, island, Australia, Statue of Liberty, Gateway Arch, Eiffel Tower, Skyscraper, England
symbol: plus sign, dove, peace symbol, peace sign, flag, Statue of Liberty, Gateway Arch, Eiffel Tower, eagle
country: Egypt, Australia, England
bird: penguin, dove, bird bath, eagle, ostrich
landmark: Statue of Liberty, Gateway Arch, Eiffel Tower

page 69
buildings: igloo, grocery store, skyscraper, hospital
famous inventions: light bulb, assembly line, personal computer, telephone
Presidents: Wilson, Roosevelt, Clinton, Reagan
natural resources: solar energy, coal, oil, forests

North American countries: Canada, Mexico, U.S.A., Guatemala
pollutants: smog, dust, noise, smoke
school subjects: History, Geography, Geometry, Science
containers: basket, closet, vase, refrigerator

page 70
natural disasters: flood, tornado, drought, earthquake
U.S. states: Florida, Ohio, Oregon, Maryland
appliances: microwave, stove, refrigerator, washing machine
beverages: water, coffee, milk, orange juice
types of music: jazz, rock and roll, classical, rap
emotions: pride, guilt, excitement, joy
rivers: Amazon, Nile, Mississippi, Snake
clothing materials: cotton, denim, wool, leather

page 71
furniture: desk, table, sofa, dresser
oceans: Atlantic, Indian, Arctic, Pacific
time words: century, decade, second, week
measurements: centimeter, inch, mile, pound
punctuation: apostrophe, dash, comma, quotation mark
hobbies: stamp collecting, writing, camping, rock climbing
communication devices: fax machine, cell phone, satellite, E-mail
relatives: cousin, nephew, aunt, wife

page 73
1. wetter
2. more careful
3. nicer
4. more interesting
5. The assignment was more difficult than the last one.
6. Her opinion was more correct than mine.
7. Visiting the dentist made him more nervous than visiting the doctor.
8. more
9. more
10. er
11. more
12. ger

page 74
1. sharpest
2. sunniest
3. most interesting
4. most popular
5. That is the dullest knife we own.
6. That movie was the most boring thing I've seen all year.
7. Carrots are the healthiest snack I eat.
8. most
9. est
10. most
11. est
12. est

page 75
1. brighter
2. lower
3. most specific
4. more difficult
5. This is the slowest printer I have ever owned.
6. Superman was more powerful than a locomotive.
7. You used the best strategy of anyone.

Answers will vary on pages not listed.

Answer Key

8. The redwood is the world's tallest tree.
9. more
10. most
11. more
12. est
13. more

page 76
1. They live in the ocean.
2. They are creative.
3. They are fractions.
4. Something flows through them.
5. They are weekend days.
6. They are capital cities.
7. They are question words.
8. They are in the air we breathe.
9. They display information.
10. They have handles.

page 77
1. They are useful tools.
2. They use lenses to magnify.
3. People go there to learn.
4. They are measurements.
5. They are musical instruments.
6. They are three-dimensional shapes.
7. They are the largest U.S. states.
8. They are habitats.

page 78
1. The Constitution is the foundation of a nation.
2. Earth can support life.
3. They measure different things.
4. China is a country, and Los Angeles is a city.
5. They both made important discoveries.
6. Oceans contain saltwater and rivers contain freshwater.
7. A book gives you more detailed information.
8. A spider is an arachnid, not an insect.

page 86
Student answers will vary.
Following are suggested answers:
courthouse: an important building, a location, requires order, rules must be followed, where a judge works, where juries do work
sentence: includes a noun and a verb, requires order, rules must be followed, first letter capitalized, punctuation is necessary
reptile: cold-blooded, includes lizards and tortoises, have rough exteriors, made up of cells
tusk: protrudes from a walrus' mouth, protrudes from an elephant's mouth, made up of cells

page 87
Student answers will vary.
Following are suggested answers:
tank: part of a car, a type of container, can hold liquids and gases, might contain gasoline
U.S. Constitution: ensures freedom, establishes rules for government, an important document, written after the American Revolution
saliva: is a liquid, located on the surface of the tongue, makes chewing and swallowing easier, found in the mouth, consists of cells
taste bud: located on the surface of the tongue, transmits sensations to the brain, helps us experience sweet and sour, consists of cells

page 88
Student answers will vary.
Following are suggested answers:
dialogue: written with quotation marks, can grow, may be friendly, assists understanding, can be deep, a type of communication, may be unfriendly
organism: can grow, made up of cells, may be friendly, may be unfriendly, can be big or small
soil: can be deep, a type of habitat, often has layers, includes minerals and decomposing matter
prediction: an educated guess, maybe correct or incorrect, a look into the future

page 89
Student answers will vary.
Following are suggested answers:
solar energy: produces little pollution, can be warm, requires the sun, most abundant energy on Earth
Russia: has a large population, part of former Soviet Union, large country, a lot of activity goes on inside it
parasite: best to be avoided, can be part of an infestation, lives inside a host, may cause destruction, may live inside intestines
anthill: has a large population, produces little pollution, often cone-shaped, a type of nest, a lot of activity goes on inside it.

Answers will vary on pages not listed.

Answer Key

page 94
1. a flightless bird
2. person, place, or thing
3. state of matter that is not liquid or gas
4. capital of the U.S.A.
5. three-horned dinosaur
6. long-legged insect
7. brown soda
8. liberty and independence
9. a vote to choose leaders
10. loud, energetic music
11. warm, heavy type of shirt
12. legless reptile
13. informational resource
14. number after 2
15. world's most popular sport

page 99
- *word:* **movie**
  description: shown on a large screen
  category: form of entertainment
  example: TV
- *word:* **quartz**
  description: used to make glass
  category: mineral
  example: mica
- *word:* **box**
  description: usually made of cardboard
  category: storage container
  example: cabinet
- *word:* **tennis**
  description: played on a large court
  category: racquet sport
  example: badminton
- *word:* **water**
  description: clear and tasteless
  category: liquid
  example: milk

- *word:* **Asia**
  description: located in Western Hemisphere
  category: continent
  example: Europe
- *word:* **aphid**
  description: damages house plants
  category: insect
  example: ladybug
- *word:* **tropical**
  description: warm year-round
  category: climate
  example: polar

page 100
- *word:* **microscope**
  description: lets you see tiny objects
  category: optical device
  example: telescope
- *word:* **medal**
  description: piece of metal on a ribbon
  category: award
  example: trophy
- *word:* **hyena**
  description: lives on African savannah
  category: small pack animal
  example: dingo
- *word:* **hurricane**
  description: high winds and surf
  category: natural disaster
  example: earthquake
- *word:* **barometric pressure**
  description: measurement of air pressure
  category: meteorology
  example: humidity
- *word:* **subway**
  description: underground train
  category: public transportation
  example: bus

- *word:* **book**
  description: contains a long story
  category: written material
  example: newspaper
- *word:* **space shuttle**
  description: reusable Earth orbiter
  category: spacecraft
  example: Apollo lunar lander

page 101
- *word:* **quotation mark**
  description: used to show dialogue
  category: punctuation mark
  example: apostrophe
- *word:* **lever**
  description: long bar that makes work easier
  category: simple machine
  example: pulley
- *word:* **Alice**
  description: had adventures in Wonderland
  category: book character
  example: Harry Potter
- *word:* **adjective**
  description: describes a noun
  category: part of speech
  example: adverb
- *word:* **vision**
  description: process of seeing
  category: sense
  example: touch
- *word:* **Civil War**
  description: conflict between the states
  category: U.S. war
  example: World War II
- *word:* **Eric the Red**
  description: Viking seaman
  category: explorer
  example: Marco Polo

Answers will vary on pages not listed.

Answer Key

- *word:* **judicial**
  description: reviews laws
  category: branch of government
  example: legislative

page 103
1. f
2. a
3. b
4. h
5. g
6. c
7. e
8. d

page 104
1. f
2. b
3. c
4. e
5. h
6. d
7. a
8. g

page 105
1. h
2. a
3. b
4. d
5. c
6. e
7. f
8. g

page 106
1. f
2. g
3. b
4. d
5. a
6. h
7. e
8. c

page 107
1. Friday
2. magnify
3. memorize
4. percent
5. subtract
6. garbage can/wastebasket
7. 8:30
8. covering
9. hot/summer
10. verb

page 108
1. clean
2. twists/curves
3. work
4. lazy/tired
5. illness/sickness/disease
6. damage
7. Money
8. colors
9. grandmother
10. study

page 109
1. The Earth's atmosphere has many layers.
2. Colin was stung by a wasp.
3. Throw that smelly banana peel away!
4. Gutenberg invented the printing press around 1450.
5. They don't like classical music.
6. Martin Luther King, Jr., was a great speaker.
7. He selected *The Adventures of Huckleberry Finn* for his book report.
8. Don moved here from Hawaii.
9. Jeanine researched her report using the Internet.

page 110
1. The ambulance took her to the hospital yesterday.
2. My birthday is January ninth.
3. According to the thermometer, this is one of the hottest days of the year.
4. Dinosaurs have been extinct for millions of years.
5. World War II ended in 1945.
6. That sentence needs a comma between the clauses.
7. We have to write a ten-page research report by Monday.
8. Both oil and mercury can harm the environment.

page 111
1. The Civil War divided the United States during the 1860s.
2. Palm trees only grow in warm, tropical climates.
3. The hot air balloon went right over our house.
4. No one permanently lives in Antarctica.
5. You will lose five points for not signing your paper.
6. Magnetism causes some objects to be attracted to one another.
7. Giant squids may be the largest ocean animals.
8. We had one hour to finish the test.

page 112
The following words might replace the words in italics in the sentences:
1. help
2. tropical plants
3. jet
4. land masses
5. animal doctor, internal pest
6. war between the states
7. hand her, box
8. New Year's Eve
9. king
10. nervous, beginning

Answers will vary on pages not listed.

References

Dempster, F., & Farris, R. (1990). The spacing effect: Research and practice. *Journal of Research and Development in Education* 23(2), 97-101

Farndon, John (1992). *Children's encyclopedia.* London: Harper Collins

Nippold, Marilyn A. (1998). *Later language development: The school-age years and adolescent years.* Austin, TX: Pro-Ed.

Pratt, C. & Grieve, R. (1984). The development of metalinguistic awareness: An introduction. In W. Tunmer, C. Pratt, & M. Herriman (Eds.), *Metalinguistic awareness in children: Theory, research, and implications* (pp.2-35). New York: Springer-Verlag.

Tibbets, Donald F. (1995). *Language intervention: Beyond the primary grades for clinicians, by clinicians.* Austin, TX: Pro-Ed.

Terban, Marvin (1993). *Checking your grammar.* New York: Scholastic Inc.

19-04-987654321